"Jesus Christ said: 'God, ov us a will so that we could c serve Him or Satan. You see, His people. Satan deceives many into followiπg ..... but hell was made for Satan and his angels. It is not my desire, nor that of My Father, that anyone should perish.' Tears of compassion ran down Jesus' cheeks." (Baxter, *A Divine Revelation of Hell*, 63).

"Jesus said, 'Hell is shaped like a human body, lying in the center of the earth. The body is lying on her back, with both arms and both legs stretched out. As I have a body of believers, so hell has a body of sin and death. As the Christ-body is built up daily, so the hell-body is also built up daily'" (Baxter, 63).

"Angelica looked down and saw a deep chasm covered in flames. They [she and Jesus] started to ascend into this abyss. She saw demons of all types, large and small . . . Jesus wept much when explaining how demons deceive people so that people will end up in hell for eternity" (Peralta, *Hell Testimonies*).

Angelica Zambrano

"Wiese . . . appeared next to an enormous pit with raging flames, raining fire, and an unbearable heat. He could see people in the flames, desperately trying to claw their way out. Their screams were 'deafening and relentless' . . . To the right of the large inferno, Wiese could see thousands of small pits, as far as he could see" (Wiese, *23 Minutes in Hell*).

Bill Wiese

"They came to a cell which had a woman . . . She screamed with groans and moans. She asked for help because her whole being was burning in flames . . . Brenes saw people burning in flames, with bodies that were a dark gray color. They moaned and shouted in pain and terror. Their flesh melted and fell from their bodies. Their skin fell from their bodies until they were just dark gray bones" (Peralta).

Carmelo Brenes

"Choo knew she was standing at the brink of hell. Jesus did not have to tell her. It was even more horrible than the description the Bible gives [see Revelation 20:13-15].

"The flames would leap unexpectedly from all directions. People would move away from flames, and as soon as they thought they were safe, another fire would burst forth. There was no rest for these unfortunate victims. They were doomed to spend all eternity being scorched and burned as they tried to escape. Choo asked who the people are. Jesus said: 'My daughter, these people did not know Me.' Jesus made this statement with a voice that heaved with grief" (Peralta).

Choo Thomas

"About 2,000 feet from the lake, Michael faced unbearable, unbelievable, all-consuming pain. His body felt like it was on fire. Yet, he was fully aware of everything transpiring around him. If anything, his five senses were more alive than ever before. He could see on the lake's surface little black objects bobbing up and down like fishing corks.

Yeager writes: 'I am not embellishing in the least. If anything, I find myself at a loss to fully express what hell is really like . . . it was more real than the flesh and blood world I live in . . . my experience was both physical and literal. It was not a vision or a dream. I could touch, taste, see, smell, and hear all that transpired. My five senses and my emotional, mental, and psychological perceptions were even more alive in the encounter than they are now'" (Yeager, *Hell is For Real*).

Michael Yeager

Hagin noticed what was causing the light. Out in front of him, beyond the gates or the entrance to hell, he saw giant, great orange flames with a white crest.

He was pulled toward hell just like a magnet pulls metal into itself. He knew that once he had entered through those gates, he could not come back (Hagin, *I Saw Hell*).

Kenneth Hagin

'I cannot vividly describe hell and the sufferings of its occupants. The words to use to describe the nature of hell and the degree of the torments and sufferings of its victims are not available to man on earth.'

People were crying and gnashing their teeth. It seemed like people were swimming inside flames of hell. He saw the burning flames of fire with people in them – men, women, children; educated, uneducated, rich, poor. Their breathing looked and sounded like someone gasping for air in his dying moment. There is no air in hell, so they are breathing in the flame of fire. The remembrance of their opportunities to accept Jesus Christ as Savior adds to their torment and sorrow (Peralta).

Thomas Sambo

"I cannot describe to you the horror of that place. I am convinced that there is no other place in the entire universe as bad as that place. The place was extremely large. I had the sense that it was expanding all the time. It was a place of utmost darkness, and the heat of it could not be measured: it was hotter than the hottest of fires . . . [There were] flies of all sizes – green, black, and gray flies . . . There were also short, thick, black worms everywhere, climbing on everything. The worms started to climb on us, and the flies were also all over us. The place was filled with the most disgusting stench; there are no words to describe the intensity of the stench. The smell was almost like rotten meat but was a hundred times worse than the most decaying meat . . . The place was filled with the noise of wailing and gnashing of teeth, as well as of demonic, evil laughter" (Peralta).

Victoria Nehale

"'Man cannot understand the nature of the torments of hell. However, go and tell him. Tell him if all the sufferings of the earth were gathered together to be borne by one man, it would still not compare to what that man will suffer for 24 hours in hell'" (Peralta).

Jesus Christ to Thomas Sambo

From *A Divine Revelation of Hell*, by Mary Baxter:
"The Lord's face was sorrowful, and His eyes were filled with great tenderness and deep love. Though those in hell were forever lost, I knew that He still loved them and would for all eternity" (Baxter, 37).

"Jesus said, 'You have all your senses in hell, and they are a lot stronger there'" (42).

"Jesus said, 'My word is true, and it declares that all must repent and turn from their sins and ask Me to come into their lives if they are to escape this place.

Through My blood there is forgiveness of sins. I am faithful and just and will forgive all those who come to Me. I will not cast them out'" (44-45).

"'Child, it is not the Father's will that anyone perish. Satan deceives many, and they follow him. But God is forgiving. He is a God of love. If these had truly come unto the Father and repented, he would have forgiven them'" (49).

"'I call different ones for different purposes in My body. But if a man or woman, boy or girl doesn't want My Spirit, I will depart'" (54).

"'We will soon be to the belly of hell. This part of hell is seventeen miles high and three miles around like a circle'" (65).

"'My child, it is better to have never known Me than to know Me and turn back from serving Me'" (72).

"Jesus said, 'Child, Satan is both the deceiver on earth and the tormentor of souls in hell. Many of the demonic powers seen here also go up to the earth at times to hurt, afflict, and deceive. **I am going to show you things that have never before been seen in this much detail . . .**'" (78).

"'Satan uses many traps and snares to deceive God's people. I will show you many of the cunning and insidious tricks of the devil'" (79).

"Jesus: 'Just as the true gospel is preached to us by a real minister, so Satan has his counterfeit ministers . . . Satan's evil gifts are like the opposite side of the coin to the spiritual gifts Jesus bestows upon believers. This is the power of darkness. These workers of Satan work in the occult, the witchcraft shops, as palm readers, and in many other ways. A medium of Satan is a powerful Satanic worker . . .'" (91)

"'Satan still thinks he can overthrow God and disrupt God's plan, but he was defeated at the cross. I took the keys away from Satan, and I have all power in heaven and in earth'" (92).

Mary writes: "I saw things in hell that are too horrible to tell . . . I also saw things that God would not let me write" (95).

"Jesus said, 'My salvation is free. Whoever will, let him come and be saved from this place of everlasting punishment. I will not cast him out . . . even if you have a written agreement with the devil, My power will break it, and My shed blood will save you'" (101).

"Jesus said, 'Satan uses many devices to destroy good men and women. He works day and night, trying to get people to serve him. If you fail to choose to serve God, you have chosen to serve the devil. Choose life, and the truth will set you free'" (149).

HELL

13 TESTIMONIES
FROM A REAL PLACE

Also from Bridge Books:

HELL

13 TESTIMONIES
FROM A REAL PLACE

JIM HARWELL

Bridge Books

Atlanta · Chicago · Nashville

Bridge Books
www.bridgebooks.org
www.bridgeministries.org
hello@bridgeministries.org

Bridge Books Subsidiary Rights Department
4487 Post Place
Nashville, Tenn. 37205

For information about Bridge Books products, books, packages, and special discounts for bulk purchases, please contact Bridge at info@bridgebooks.org.

Scripture references are taken from the New King James Version. © Thomas Nelson, Inc. 1992.

Cover designed by Alexandre Rito
Hell Diagram by Dean Tomasek and Jim Harwell

Manufactured in the United States of America

10 9 8 7 6 5 4 3 2 1

Library of Congress

ISBN-13: 978-0-9986819-0-0
ISBN-10:   0-9986819-0-0

Contents

	Introduction	
1	"Hell & It's Chambers" Diagram	19
2	Mary Baxter	22
	Highlights, Revelations & Truths	23
	Left Leg of Hell	29
	Right Leg of Hell	33
	The Pits of Hell	37
	The Tunnel of Fear	41
	Activity in Hell	43
	The Belly of Hell	46
	The Cells in Hell	48
	The Horrors of Hell	50
	The Heart of Hell	53
	Outer Darkness	56
	The Center of Hell	58
	List of Lost Souls from Visits to Hell	61
3	Kenneth Hagin	64
4	Michael Yeager	68
5	Curtis Kelley	72
6	Ron Regan	74
7	Carmelo Brenes	77
8	Mario Martinez	80
9	Thomas Sambo	83
10	Choo Thomas	87
11	Bill Wiese	91
12	Victoria Nehale	96
13	Bernarda Fernandez	102
14	Angelica Zambrano	104
15	Every Scripture about Hell & the Underworld	108
16	Number of People Per Day Who Die and Go to Hell	125
17	The Five Worlds Under the Earth	128
	Notes and Bibliography	137

Introduction

If you read/listen to only one thing in this book, please read this: hell is a real place, a place of fire, torment, torture, and indescribable horror, far beyond human comprehension. Those in hell will endure unimaginable suffering, forever.

In hell, lost souls burn in fire forever. Their flesh literally burns and falls off their bodies. Worms and maggots crawl inside them. It is a place of continual loud wailing, weeping, screaming, and gnashing of teeth.

They feel and know everything going on.

Those in hell suffer a literal eternal death. Human beings exist forever, because we are spirit beings.

If you do not believe me, read Jesus Christ's words about hell in the Gospels: Matthew 5:22,29,30; 10:28; 11:23; 12:40; 16:18; 18:9; 23:15; 23:33; 25:41; Mark 9:44,46,48; and Luke 16:19-31 (see pages 119-123).

Hell is currently located in the center of the earth.

A person in hell has ALL their senses – sight, smell, hearing, taste, and touch – and all five are a lot stronger in hell. The spirit realm is on a much higher level than the natural realm.

This book contains the testimonies of 13 people who have been to hell and have come back to earth. They all describe the same scary, horrifying, terrifying, and shocking place.

Even if we did not have these and other modern testimonies, there are more than 110 specific scriptures in the Bible about hell and the other four worlds under the earth, which are: the pit, tartarus, the lake of fire, and paradise (see page 128 for a summary of them).

Hell is written about often in both the Old and New Testaments. Jesus preached and talked about hell more often than He spoke about heaven.

Every scripture about hell in the Bible is in this book, from page 108 to 124.

Who goes to hell?

Anyone on earth who dies and does not know Jesus Christ as their personal Lord and Savior will go to hell and spend their eternity there.

Eternity

Eternity. Forever.

Eternity's importance and significance cannot be put into human words.

It's forever. And ever . . .

Every person will exist eternally, either in heaven or hell; either in eternal life or eternal death.

Eternity is infinitely more important than any length of human time, whether 75 years, 6,000 years, or 4.5 billion years, an estimated age of the earth.

It only makes sense that we as humans should live in light of eternity.

Our life on earth is just a vapor, a mist that appears for a little while and then is gone.

The Father God Almighty and the Lord Jesus Christ want everyone to have everlasting life and make it to heaven. They do not want anyone to spend eternity in hell. Man has a free will. God cannot make anyone follow Him.

Hell

In hell, there is no life of any kind – no living things, no light, no love, no mercy, no water, no food. There is nothing good at all.

Hell is a place of: extreme darkness; awful nauseating smells; scary, massive overpowering demons that torture helpless people; worms and maggots that crawl inside people and never die; and worse.

Anyone who ends up in hell can never get out, FOREVER. For ETERNITY. At death, judgment is set.

The beings in hell are: demons; some of the angels; Satan (a fallen angel); and, tragically, humans who died without knowing Jesus Christ as their Lord and Savior, without having a personal relationship with God Almighty through His Son Jesus Christ through the Holy Spirit.

Humans in hell can never get out.

Judgment is set. It can never be changed, FOREVER.

They are stuck in hell for eternity, and they know it. They are placed in small pits or cells. Their bodies are continually burned with fire and hot coals. The fire and flames literally burn and tear their flesh off their skeletons.

Many worms and maggots crawl inside them and are not affected by the fire. Demons torment and torture them and keep them in their holding places.

Humans in hell feel everything and know everything going on. They remember their life on earth and the many times they could have repented and received Jesus Christ. They remember the times they could have done good and did not. They remember family and friends on earth – and hope that they avoid hell.

They know they are among billions of other lost

souls, all of them weeping and wailing in torment. Approximately 108 billion people have lived so far on earth – and most people do not make it to heaven.

People in hell only leave their small pit or cell to be taken somewhere else for even worse torture, sometimes by Satan himself.

When the earth is destroyed, hell will be thrown into the Lake of Fire, where everyone in hell will burn in fire FOREVER (Revelation 20:14).

Why is there a hell?

Why is there even a place with such horrible, extreme, excruciating suffering?

We know only in part.

The word of God says that hell was "prepared for the devil and his angels" (Matthew 25:41) – not for man.

The real battle in the universe is between God Almighty – the Father, Son, and Holy Spirit – and His enemy, Satan.

The devil was originally the highest-ranking angel (Lucifer; see Isaiah 14 and Ezekiel 28) who rebelled and tried to overthrow God. Satan was cast out of heaven and is still today opposing and trying to defeat God. He still thinks he can overthrow God, but he was defeated at the cross of Jesus Christ.

One of the main ways He opposes God is by deceiving human beings into NOT following God through Jesus Christ – and into following the devil, or any other path apart from Jesus Christ.

Satan and his enslaved demons hate people, because people are made in God's image; and Satan hates God.

Why is this happening? This battle is a mystery in many ways to humans. But God has revealed much about it through His word. See the book *War in the*

Heavens for a full summary of the real war in the universe.

This battle has been going on for a long time – we do not know how long.

When you understand the spiritual battle and the good and evil forces behind it, a lot of questions and mysteries are answered and solved.

Tragically, Satan deceives people into following him – and those who follow him will end up in hell. It's very important to know this: if someone is not following Jesus Christ, that person is following and serving Satan, the devil. Every person on earth is in one of two families: God's or the devil's.

Description of hell – continued

For the billions of lost souls in hell, there is no relief from the suffering – no rest, no sleep, no water or food of any kind, no compassion from anyone. Remember, the good things we have on earth are not in hell. For a full explanation of this, see page 95.

There is a continual foul, toxic stench and odor from the decaying flesh, garbage, and much more.

No human would even want to see hell or spend one second or minute there, let alone eternity.

Tragically, it is estimated that more than 83,000 people a day – and possibly more than 100,000 – die and end up in hell (fully explained on pages 125-127).

Where is hell? It is in the center of the earth. Hell is shaped like a human body lying on its back, with arms and legs stretched out. Hell is beneath those on earth, which is why the Bible refers to hell as "under" and "beneath" (Deuteronomy 32:22 and Isaiah 14:9).

There are many different parts of hell, such as the arms, belly, heart, head, legs, and so forth. In recent years, Jesus has revealed much about hell through his children. Those revelations are the main subject of this book.

A major portion of this book is a summary of perhaps the most detailed and thorough description and revelation of hell, which is found in Mary Baxter's book *A Divine Revelation of Hell*. The quote below is from that book.

The truth about hell is scary, shocking, tragic, and more much.

Jesus Christ: **"I came to save all men. I desire that all who are lost will repent and call upon My name. It is not My will that any should perish, but have everlasting life. Sad to say, most will not repent of their sins before they die, and they will go to hell. But the way to heaven is the same for all people. You must be born again to enter the kingdom of God. You must come to the Father in My name and repent of your sins. You must sincerely give your heart to God and serve Him"** (94).

HELL & ITS CHAMBERS

"THE **FURNACE OF FIRE**...WAILING & GNASHING OF TEETH." MT 13:50

"THE **EVERLASTING FIRE** PREPARED FOR THE DEVIL & HIS ANGELS." MT 25:41

"WHERE THEIR WORM DOES NOT DIE & THE **FIRE IS NOT QUENCHED**." MARK 9:44

"YOU HAVE ALL YOUR SENSES IN HELL, & THEY ARE A LOT STRONGER THERE." JESUS CHRIST

"A **FIRE SHALL BURN** TO THE LOWEST HELL." DEUT 32:22

"HELL FROM BENEATH." ISAIAH 14:9

"HELL IS SHAPED LIKE A HUMAN BODY, LYING IN THE CENTER OF THE EARTH, ON HER BACK, ARMS & LEGS STRETCHED OUT." JESUS CHRIST

OUTER DARKNESS

CAST INTO OUTER DARK- NESS. THERE WILL BE WEEP- ING & GNASH- ING OF TEETH. MT 8:12, 22:13, 25:30

"HELL HAS ENLARGED ITSELF." ISAIAH 5:14

"IN HELL, WHERE HE WAS IN TORMENT.." LK 16:23

"FEAR HIM WHO HAS THE POWER TO CAST INTO HELL." LK 12:5

"GOD, OUR FATHER, GAVE EACH OF US A WILL SO THAT WE COULD CHOOSE WHETHER WE WOULD SERVE HIM OR SA- TAN." JESUS CHRIST

GATEWAYS TO HELL: GIANT FUNNELS, FROM THE SKIES TO THE EARTH TO HELL HOW BEINGS TRAVEL IN THE SPIRIT REALMS

HORNS, OR BRANCHES, FROM THE HEART OF HELL, SPILL EVIL ONTO THE EARTH; THEY REPRE- SENT EVIL KINGDOMS ON EARTH DANIEL 7,8

THE 5 WORLDS UNDER THE EARTH:
HELL, OR SHEOL
THE PIT: abode of demons
TARTARUS: fallen angels in chains
LAKE OF FIRE: hell's final location
PARADISE: pre-ascension saints

"DEATH & HELL WERE CAST INTO THE **LAKE OF FIRE & SULFUR**. THIS IS THE SECOND DEATH. ANYONE NOT FOUND WRITTEN IN THE BOOK OF LIFE WAS CAST INTO THE **LAKE OF FIRE**." REVELATION 20:14-15; 21:8

"WIDE IS THE GATE & BROAD IS THE WAY THAT LEADS TO DESTRUCTION, & THERE ARE MANY WHO GO IN BY IT." MT 7:13

HELL'S PLACES & LOCATIONS

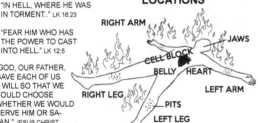

RIGHT ARM

JAWS

CELL BLOCK

BELLY   HEART

LEFT ARM

RIGHT LEG

PITS

LEFT LEG

SOULS IN PITS: ANYONE WHO DIES WITHOUT KNOWING JESUS CHRIST AS LORD & SAVIOR

SOULS IN THE CELL BLOCK: EVIL PEOPLE W/ FAMILIAR SPIRITS, HOMOSEXUALS, LESBIANS, ADULTERERS, SORCERERS, MEDIUMS, SOOTHSAYERS, DIVINERS, DRUG PEDDLERS, IDOL WORSHIPERS, PALM READ- ERS, WITCHES, WARLOCKS

"I CAME TO SAVE ALL MEN. I DESIRE THAT ALL WHO ARE LOST WILL REPENT & CALL UPON MY NAME. IT IS NOT MY WILL THAT ANY SHOULD PERISH. SAD TO SAY, MOST WILL NOT REPENT OF THEIR SINS BEFORE THEY DIE, & THEY WILL GO TO HELL. THE WAY TO HEAVEN IS THE SAME FOR ALL PEOPLE. YOU MUST BE BORN AGAIN. YOU MUST COME TO THE FATHER IN MY NAME & REPENT OF YOUR SINS. YOU MUST SINCERELY GIVE YOUR HEART TO GOD & SERVE HIM." JESUS CHRIST

References: Holy Bible NKJV; *Divine Revelation of Hell*, Baxter

HELL & ITS CHAMBERS

"THE **EVERLASTING FIRE** PREPARED FOR THE DEVIL & HIS ANGELS."

"THE **FURNACE OF FIRE**...WAILING & GNASHING OF TEETH."

"THEIR WORM DOES NOT DIE & THE **FIRE IS NOT QUENCHED.**"

"HELL IS SHAPED LIKE A HUMAN BODY, LYING IN THE CENTER OF THE EARTH, ON HER BACK, ARMS & LEGS STRETCHED OUT."

"YOU HAVE ALL YOUR SENSES IN HELL, & THEY ARE A LOT STRONGER THERE." JESUS CHRIST

MT 25:41
MT 13:50
MK 9:44

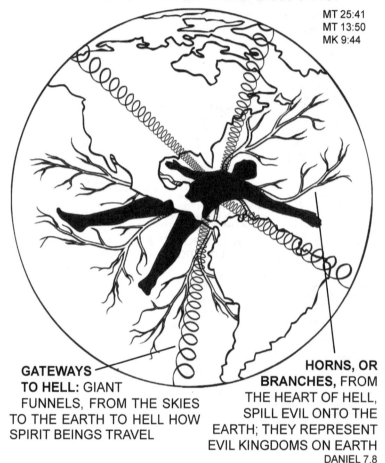

GATEWAYS TO HELL: GIANT FUNNELS, FROM THE SKIES TO THE EARTH TO HELL HOW SPIRIT BEINGS TRAVEL

HORNS, OR BRANCHES, FROM THE HEART OF HELL, SPILL EVIL ONTO THE EARTH; THEY REPRESENT EVIL KINGDOMS ON EARTH

DANIEL 7,8

"DEATH & HELL WERE CAST INTO THE **LAKE OF FIRE & SULFUR**. THIS IS THE SECOND DEATH. ANYONE NOT FOUND WRITTEN IN THE BOOK OF LIFE WAS CAST INTO THE **LAKE OF FIRE.**" REVELATION 20:14-15; 21:8

HELL'S PLACES & LOCATIONS

"A **FIRE SHALL BURN** TO THE LOWEST HELL." DEUT 32:22

"HELL HAS ENLARGED ITSELF." ISAIAH 5:14

"IN HELL, WHERE HE WAS IN TORMENT.." LK 16:23

"FEAR HIM WHO HAS THE PWR TO CAST INTO HELL."LK12:5

"GOD, OUR FATHER, GAVE EACH OF US A WILL SO THAT WE COULD CHOOSE WHETH-ER WE WOULD SERVE HIM OR SATAN." JESUS CHRIST

SOULS IN PITS: ANYONE WHO DIES WITHOUT KNOWING JESUS CHRIST AS LORD & SAVIOR

SOULS IN THE CELL BLOCK: EVIL PEOPLE W/ FMILIAR SPIRITS, HOMOSEXUALS, LESBIANS, ADUL-TERERS, SORCERERS, MEDIUMS, SOOTHSAYERS, DIVINERS, DRUG PEDDLERS, IDOL WORSHIPERS, PALM READRS, WITCHES, WAR-LOCKS

RIGHT ARM · JAWS

CELL BLOCK

THE BELLY · HEART

LEFT ARM

RIGHT LEG

PITS

LEFT LEG

THE 5 WORLDS UNDER THE EARTH: HELL, THE PIT, TARTA-RUS, LAKE OF FIRE, PARADISE

CAST INTO OUTER DARKNESS. THERE WILL BE WEEPING & GNASHING OF TEETH MT 8:12, 22:13

"I CAME TO SAVE ALL MEN. I DESIRE THAT ALL WHO ARE LOST WILL REPENT & CALL UPON MY NAME...SAD TO SAY, MOST WILL NOT REPENT OF THEIR SINS BEFORE THEY DIE, & THEY WILL GO TO HELL. THE WAY TO HEAVEN IS THE SAME FOR ALL PEOPLE. YOU MUST BE BORN AGAIN. YOU MUST COME TO THE FATHER IN MY NAME & REPENT OF YOUR SINS. YOU MUST SINCERELY GIVE YOUR HEART TO GOD & SERVE HIM." JESUS CHRIST

References: Holy Bible NKJV; *Divine Revelation of Hell*, Baxter

ONE

Mary Baxter

In 1976, Jesus took a young American woman Mary Baxter on a 40-night tour of hell and commissioned her to tell others about it.

Her book *A Divine Revelation of Hell* (Whitaker House, 1993) is the story of her visits to hell and heaven and her visions and revelations. Baxter has written numerous other books about heaven, angels, the spirit realm, and more.

Jesus showed Baxter hell in perhaps the most detail hell has ever been revealed. He told her: "'I am going to show you things that have never before been seen in this much detail . . .'"[1] The book contains many deep truths, revelations, and visions that confirm the Bible and God's plan for humanity.

The first portion of the summary below contains some of the most important portions of the book. The next section is a summary of the incredible book.

Highlights, revelations and deep truths . . .

"The Lord's face was sorrowful, and His eyes were filled with great tenderness and deep love. Though those in hell were forever lost, I knew that He still loved them and would for all eternity" (Baxter, 37).

"Jesus said: 'My child, God, our Father, gave each one of us a will so that we could choose whether we would serve Him or Satan. You see, God did not make hell for His people. Satan deceives many into following him, but hell was made for Satan and his angels. It is not my desire, nor that of My Father, that anyone should perish.' Tears of compassion ran down Jesus' cheeks.

"Jesus explained that He has all power in heaven and on earth. He explained that they would at times be seen by the evil forces and lost souls and at other times they would not be" (38).

"Jesus said, 'You have all your senses in hell, and they are a lot stronger there'" (42).

"Jesus said, 'My word is true, and it declares that all must repent and turn from their sins and ask Me to come into their lives if they are to escape this place. Through My blood there is forgiveness of sins. I am faithful and just and will forgive all those who come to Me. I will not cast them out'" (44-45).

"'Child, it is not the Father's will that anyone perish. Satan deceives many, and they follow him. But God is forgiving. He is a God of love. If these had truly come unto the Father and repented, He would have forgiven them'" (49).

"Jesus said, 'Many in the last days will depart from the faith, giving heed to seducing spirits and will serve sin. Come out from among them, and be separate. Walk not in the way with them'" (52).

"'I call different ones for different purposes in My body. But if a man or woman, boy or girl doesn't want My Spirit, I will depart'" (54).

Jesus said, "'The world and all that is in it will pass away, but My words will not pass away'" (60).

Jesus said, "'Hell is shaped like a human body lying in the center of the earth. The body is lying on her back, with both arms and both legs stretched out. As I have a body of believers, so hell has a body of sin and death. As the Christ-body is built up daily, so the hell-body is also built up daily'" (63).

"'We will soon be to the belly of hell. This part of hell is seventeen miles high and three miles around like a circle'" (65).

"'My child, it is better to have never known Me than to know Me and turn back from serving Me'" (72).

"Jesus said, 'Child, Satan is both the deceiver on earth and the tormentor of souls in hell. Many of the demonic powers seen here also go up to the earth at times to hurt, afflict, and deceive. I am going to show you things that have never before been seen in this much detail . . .'" (78).

"'Satan uses many traps and snares to deceive God's people. I will show you many of the cunning and insidious tricks of the devil'" (79).

Jesus: "'Just as the true gospel is preached to us by a real minister, so Satan has his counterfeit ministers . . . Satan's evil gifts are like the opposite side of the coin to the spiritual gifts Jesus bestows upon believers. This is the power of darkness. These workers of Satan work in the occult, the witchcraft shops, as palm readers, and in many other ways. A medium of Satan is a powerful Satanic worker . . .'" (91).

"'Satan still thinks he can overthrow God and disrupt God's plan, but he was defeated at the cross. I took the keys away from Satan, and I have all power in heaven and in earth'" (92).

As horrible as her descriptions are, Mary saw things in hell that are too horrible to tell. She writes: "I saw things in hell that are too horrible to tell . . . I also saw things that God would not let me write" (95).

Jesus: "'Satan feeds on evil. He glories in pain and suffering and gains power from it'" (99).

Jesus: "'My salvation is free. Whoever will, let him come and be saved from this place of everlasting punishment. I will not cast him out'" (100).

Jesus: "'These branches, which look like arteries of a heart, are pipelines that go up through the earth to spill out evil upon it. These are the horns that Daniel saw, and they represent evil kingdoms on the earth.

Some have already been, some shall be, and some are now. Evil kingdoms will arise, and the Antichrist will rule over many people, places, and things. If possible, the very elect will be deceived by him. Many will turn away and worship the beast and his image.

"'Out of these main branches or horns, smaller branches will grow. Out of the smaller branches will come demons, evil spirits and all manner of evil forces. They will be released upon the earth and instructed by Satan to do many evil works. These kingdoms and evil forces will obey the beast, and many will follow him to destruction. It is here in the heart of hell that these things begin'" (105).

Jesus: "'Satan uses many devices to destroy good men and women. He works day and night, trying to get people to serve him. If you fail to choose to serve God, you have chosen to serve the devil. Choose life, and the truth will set you free'" (149).

Mary Baxter has long been a dedicated prayer warrior. Jesus chose her for a special calling to warn people about hell. Jesus explained to her that He would be showing her hell in detail that had never been seen before. Usually in the middle of the night, Jesus and Baxter would leave her home and family and go to hell. Baxter would visit hell in her spirit person, the real and eternal person of a human. Just like God, a human is a three-in-one being: a spirit, a soul (mind, will, and emotions), and a body.

They walked through many of the parts of hell and saw the unimaginable horrors, suffering, and torment of the lost souls there. Jesus wept numerous times as

they talked to lost souls. Baxter also wept and mourned. She was in great fear and trembling while there and
after her experiences.

Jesus taught Baxter about hell and various aspects
of the forces of evil. He taught her about the different
parts of hell, how demons function, and the various
locations of pits and cells where souls are kept impris-
oned for eternity. They saw demons at work and Satan
tormenting people. They actually spoke to 19 specific
people lost in hell (summary is on pages 62-63), people
from various centuries and times of history.

Jesus explained to her that man has a complete free
will and chooses whom he or she serves. He taught
her that God cannot make anyone serve Him or follow
Him. God made man into His own image and gave
man a complete free will.

Jesus taught Baxter many deep spiritual truths. He
gave her incredible revelations about the spirit realm
and the battle between God and the devil. She received
several visions of the end times as well, such as the Return of Jesus Christ.

Jesus told her: "'Behold, My child. I am going to take
you by My Spirit into hell so that you may be able to
make a record of the reality of it, to tell the whole earth
that hell is real, and to bring the lost out of darkness
and into the light of the gospel of Jesus Christ'" (15).

One night, instantly, Baxter's spirit was taken out of
her body, and she and Jesus went up out of her room
and into the sky. Her husband and children were
asleep in their home.

Soon they were high in the heavens. Jesus was full of
glory and power, and peace flowed from Him. He told
her, "'I love you. Fear not, for I am with you'" (16).

Baxter was high above the earth. She could see what
looked like large funnels spinning around and around

down to a center point on the earth. They were scat-

tered about the earth in many places, coming up from the earth, moving continuously like dirty slinky's. Jesus explained that these funnels are gateways into hell (see Diagram: p. 20). They both entered one of the funnels. It was like a tunnel, spinning around and around.

A deep darkness descended on Baxter, along with a smell so horrible it took her breath away. The sides of the tunnel had living forms embedded in them. The evil forms were dark gray, and they moved, laughed, and cried out to Jesus and Mary as they passed the forms. Jesus explained that these forms are evil spirits ready to be spewed out onto the earth as Satan gives the orders (17).

Baxter had all her senses, and she noticed that her senses had become more sensitive than they are on earth.

As they came to the bottom of the tunnel, she could hear piercing cries and all sorts of sounds. The worst odor she had ever smelled filled the air. It was the smell of decaying flesh. She heard cries of despair. Soon she would find out that these were the cries of the dead.

She felt a gust of evil wind and a small suction force. There were lights similar to lightening and flashing strobe lights. She saw large ugly snakes slithering all around her.

Jesus explained what they were about to see and the fact that it is real.

Finally, they arrived in hell.

Baxter could see flying objects darting here and there. She heard groaning sounds and pitiful cries. The path was a dry, powdery dirt. She saw a dim light ahead. They were at the entrance to a small dark tunnel.

Mary writes: "Some things I cannot put on paper;

they were too awful to describe" (19).

The Left Leg of Hell

One of the first places they visited was the left leg of hell. Jesus explained that the left leg has many pits. The tunnel they were in branches off into other parts of hell.

"'The world must know about the reality of hell,' said Jesus. 'You have been chosen to reveal these truths to them'" (21).

Jesus revealed Himself to Baxter as a bright light, brighter than the sun. The form of a man was in the center of that light. Baxter explains that sometimes Jesus appeared as a man, while at other times He was in the form of a spirit (21).

Jesus said, "'Child, when I speak, the Father has spoken. The Father and I are one'" (22).

As they walked, evil spirits fled from the presence of Jesus.

At the top of the tunnel, doorways the size of small windows were opening and shutting very fast. Evil creatures flew by them, up and out of the gateways of hell. Baxter's senses were in full force. Fear and danger was everywhere. She was trembling was fright.

She noticed she was a spirit form, and the form was in the shape of herself.

They both stepped from the tunnel onto a path with wide swaths of land on either side. As far as she could see, there were pits of fire in the ground. The pits were shaped like bowls and were four feet across and three feet deep. Brimstone was embedded in the side of the pits and glowed red like hot coals of fire.

They looked into a pit and saw a lost soul. Fire began at the bottom of the pit, swept upward, and clothed the lost soul in flames. In a moment, the fire would die down, then with a rushing wind would sweep back over the tormented soul.

The soul was caged inside a skeleton form.

A woman cried out from the pit, "Jesus, have mercy!"

Baxter was in shock and wanted to help her, to pull her out of the pit.

Decayed flesh hung by shreds from her bones. Her eyes were gone, only the empty sockets were remaining. She had no hair.

The fire started at her feet in small flames and grew as it climbed up and over her body. She cried out, "'Lord, lord, I want out of here!'" She kept reaching out for Jesus. Worms were crawling out of her bones. The worms were not harmed by the fire (24).

The woman's cries and sobbing shook her form.

There was great sorrow on Jesus' face.

They continued on. The path was winding, twisting in and out between the pits of fire as far as Mary could see. Cries, moans, and screams were all around. The smell of dead and decaying flesh was thick.

In the next pit was a man. He said, "'Lord, have mercy on me!'" Baxter could only tell their gender when they spoke.

Great wailing sobs came from the man. He said, "'I'm so sorry, Jesus. Forgive me. Take me out of here. I have been in this place of torment for years. I beg you, let me out!'" The man was crying and sobbing deeply.

Mary looked at Jesus and saw that Jesus was also crying.

The man asked, "'Haven't I suffered enough for my sins? It's been forty years since my death'" (26).

People in hell know how long they have been there, and they can remember their life on earth.

Jesus explained to the man: "'It is written, 'The just

shall live by faith.' All mockers and unbelievers shall have their part in the lake of fire . . .'" He explained that many times, people were sent to this man to show him the way, but he would not listen and even laughed and refused the gospel. The man even mocked Jesus and would not repent.

The man then asked Jesus if the man could go tell his people that they must repent while on earth. Jesus answered: "'They have preachers, teachers, elders – all ministering the gospel. They will tell them. They also have the advantages of the modern communication systems and many other ways to learn of Me. I sent workers to them that they might believe and be saved. If they will not believe when they hear the gospel, neither will they be persuaded though one rise from the dead'" (27).

The man cursed Jesus. Flames rose up and continued burning flesh off his skeleton.

Jesus said, "'Hell is real; judgment is real. I love them so, My child . . .Tell the world for Me that hell is real, that men and women must repent of their sins'" (28).

In the next pit that they visited, there was a small-framed woman about 80 years old. The skin was removed from her bones by the continual fire, leaving only the bones with the dirty-mist soul inside, with worms crawling inside the bones.

Jesus said, "'You must know and tell the truth about hell. Heaven is real! Hell is real! Come, we must go on.'"

Mary saw the woman crying and putting her hands together as if she was praying. Mary was so sad. Though Mary was in spirit form, she herself was crying and knew the woman felt all these things also.

Jesus always knew Mary's thoughts.

"'Yes, child, they do,' He said. 'When people come

here, they have the same feelings and thoughts as when they were on earth. They remember their families and friends and all the times they had a chance to repent but refused to do so. Memory is always with them. If only they had believed the gospel and repented before it was too late'" (29).

The woman had one leg and holes in her hip bones. Jesus explained her story. As a woman, she got cancer, and surgery was done to save her life. After the surgery, she was a bitter old woman. People prayed with her and told her she could be healed. But she refused to listen. She knew Jesus at one time but in time came to hate Him. Yet Jesus still pleaded with her, wanting to help her and to heal and to bless her. She turned her back on Jesus and cursed Him. Even after she turned her back on Jesus, He still tried to draw her by His Spirit.

The woman cried out, "'Lord Jesus, please forgive me now . . . If only I had repented before it was too late! Lord, help me out of here . . . Why did I wait until too late? . . . '" (30).

The next pit contained a woman whose skeletal form was full of holes. Her bones were showing, and there were only holes where he eyes and nose had been. Her dress was torn and on fire. She was on her knees as if searching for something, clawing the sides of the pit. Fire clung to her hands, and dead flesh kept falling off her.

Sobs shook her body. "'O Lord, O Lord, I want out!'" She climbed up to the top of the pit, almost getting out, when suddenly a large demon with great wings and hair all over its form ran to her. The demon was brownish black and as big as a grizzly bear. The wings were broken and hanging down its sides. His eyes were set far back into his head. The demon rushed over and pushed the woman very hard backward into the pit and fire. Mary was heartbroken at the sight and wanted to help her.

"Jesus said, 'Judgment has been set. God has spoken.'" He went on to explain that He called and called the woman to repent, even from an early age and all her life. But she would not listen.

The woman cried out in regret, explaining that she wanted the world instead of Jesus. She got riches, fame, and fortune but could not take them with her after death. She cried, "'My sweet Lord, if only I had listened to You! I will regret that forever . . .'" (33).

She went on to confess that she knew God was calling her and drawing her with cords of love. But she used God. Over time, she began to serve Satan more and more, until she loved Satan more than God. Even then, God continued to draw her. Finally, she was killed in a car wreck. She reached out to Jesus with her bony hands.

Tears fell down Jesus' cheeks as they moved to the next pit.

Jesus explained to Mary about the location and shape of hell. He said: "'Hell has a body (like a human form) lying on her back in the center of the earth. Hell is shaped like a human body – very large and with many chambers of torment. Remember to tell the people of earth that hell is real. Millions of lost souls are here, and more are coming every day. On the Great Judgment Day, death and hell will be cast into the lake of fire; that will be the second death'" (34-35).

The Right Leg of Hell

On another night, Jesus took Baxter to the right leg. The Lord's face was sorrowful, and His eyes were filled with great tenderness and deep love. Though those in hell were forever lost, Mary knew that He still loved them and would for all eternity.

Jesus said: "'My child, God, our Father, gave each one of us a will so that we could choose whether we would serve Him or Satan. You see, God did not make hell for His people. Satan deceives many into following him, but hell was made for Satan and his angels. It is not my desire, nor that of My Father, that anyone should perish'" (38). Tears of compassion ran down Jesus' cheeks.

Jesus explained that He has all power in heaven and on earth. He explained that they would at times be seen by the evil forces and lost souls and at other times they would not be seen.

They arrived at the right leg. The stench was so repugnant Mary was sick. Darkness was everywhere except for Jesus' light and the light of the fires from the pits, which dotted the landscape as far as she could see.

Suddenly demons of all kinds, sizes, and shapes went past them, growling. A big demon gave orders to small ones, telling them to break up homes, destroy families, seduce weak Christians, and mislead people. He offered them rewards when they returned. He said, "'. . . remember, we are servants of the prince of darkness and of the powers of the air'" (39).

The large demon was as big as a large bear, brown, with a head like a bat and eyes set very far back into a hairy face. He had hairy arms, and fangs came out of the hair on his face.

Another one was small like a monkey with long arms and hair. He had a tiny face and pointed nose but no visible eyes.

They were grotesque and all shapes. One had a large head and ears and a long tail. Another was as large as a horse and had smooth skin. They had a terrible odor that made Mary sick.

They arrived at another pit. In the pit, a large-framed man was preaching the gospel.

Jesus explained that this man was a preacher while on earth and at one time served God. He was about six feet tall. Burning flesh was hanging from him, and his skull was in flames. An awful odor came from him. Somehow, his tattered clothing was still on his body; the flames did not destroy them.

The man spread his hands as if he were holding a book, and he began to read Scriptures from the make-believe book.

Jesus said to him, "'Peace, be still.'" The man turned to Jesus and began confessing his sins and wrongs. A summary:

1. He did not tell people about hell
2. He did not believe that there is a hell
3. He did not believe Jesus was coming again
4. He did not like anyone of a different race or color of skin
5. He made his own rules about heaven and right and wrong
6. He led people astray
7. He caused people to stumble over the Holy Word
8. He took money from the poor

"Jesus said, 'You not only distorted and misrepresented the Holy Word of God, but you lied about your not knowing the truth. The pleasures of life were more important to you than truth. I visited you Myself and tried to turn you around, but you would not listen. You went on your own way, and evil was your lord. You knew the truth, but you would not repent or turn back to Me. I was there all the time. I waited for you.

I wanted you to repent, but you did not. And now the judgment has been set'" (43).

"Pity was on the face of Jesus. [He spoke again], 'You should have told the truth, and you would have turned many to righteousness with God's word, which says all unbelievers will have their part in the lake that burns with fire and brimstone. You knew the way of the cross. You knew the way of righteousness. You knew to speak the truth. But Satan filled your heart with lies, and you went into sin. You should have repented with sincerity, not halfway. My word is true. It does not lie. And now it is too late, too late'" (43).

The man cursed Jesus. As they walked away, the man was still cursing Jesus.

As they walked on, the hands of the lost reached out to Jesus, and with pleading voices they called out to Him for mercy. Their bony arms and hands were gray-black from the burning, with no live flesh or blood. They had no organs, nothing living. Just death and dying.

Mary was physically weak and could hardly stand. She sobbed heavily and felt deep pity for the lost. She told Jesus she was hurting inside.

At another pit, a woman spoke to Jesus. She stood in the center of flames, which covered her body. Her bones were full of worms and dead flesh.

She raised her hands to Jesus, crying, "'Let me out of here. I will give You my heart now, Jesus. I will tell others about Your forgiveness. I will witness for You. I beg You, please let me out!'

"Jesus said, 'My word is true, and it declares that all must repent and turn from their sins and ask Me to come into their lives if they are to escape this place. Through My blood there is forgiveness of sins. I am faithful and just and will forgive all those who come to

Me. I will not cast them out'" (44).

"She asked Him, 'Lord, is there no way out of here?'

"Jesus spoke very softly. 'Woman, you were given many opportunities to repent, but you hardened your heart and would not. And you knew My word said that all whoremongers will have their part in the lake of fire'" (44-45).

"Jesus said to Mary, 'This woman had sinful affairs with many men, and she caused many homes to be broken apart. Yet through all this, I loved her still. I came to her not in condemnation but with salvation. I sent many of My servants to her that she might repent of her evil ways, but she would not . . . Satan entered her, and she grew bitter and would not forgive others . . . Part of her wanted to serve Me, but you cannot serve God and Satan at the same time. Every person must make a choice as to whom they will serve'" (45).

Mary was shaking from the horrors of hell. Jesus said, "'Peace, be still.'" Mary cried out, "I never thought that hell would be like this. When will this end?'

"'My child,' Jesus replied, 'only the Father knows when the end will come.' Then He spoke again to her, 'Peace, be still.' Great strength came upon Mary (46).

They walked on through the pits. Mary's heart broke for the lost souls. She wanted to pull each person out and rush them to the feet of Jesus.

Back home, she cried and cried. During the day she relived hell and its horror.

More Pits

The next night, Jesus and Baxter went into the right leg of hell again. Mary saw Jesus' love for the lost souls there.

"'Child, it is not the Father's will that anyone perish.

Satan deceives many, and they follow him. But God is forgiving. He is a God of love. If these had truly come unto the Father and repented, he would have forgiven them'" (49).

Mary noticed great tenderness on Jesus' face as He spoke.

As they walked along the pathway, burning hands reached out to Jesus. Their cries filled Mary's heart with a grief so great she cannot describe it.

They stopped at a pit. Inside was a woman. She cried to Jesus for deliverance.

"Jesus looked on her with love and said, 'While you were on earth, I called you to come to Me. I pleaded with you to get your heart right with me before it was too late. I visited you many times in the midnight hour to tell you of My love. I wooed you, loved you and drew you to Me by My Spirit . . .'" (50).

The woman with her lips said she loved Jesus, but her heart did not mean it. She wanted the world and not Jesus. She did not repent of her sins. She was a member of a church but had many sins. She caused others to stumble at the word. She would not forgive others. She pretended to serve God but when away from believers, she lied, cheated, and stole. She gave heed to seducing spirits and enjoyed her double life. She knew the straight and narrow way. She had a double tongue. She judged her fellow believers, believing she was holier than they were.

"'This I know, you would not listen to My sweet Spirit of compassion . . .'" (52). She judged and was a very hard person. She knew the ways of the Lord and understood. "'You played with God, and God knows all things. If you had served God, you would not be here today. You cannot serve Satan and God at the same time'" (52).

"Jesus said, 'Many in the last days will depart from the faith, giving heed to seducing spirits and will serve sin. Come out from among them, and be separate. Walk not in the way with them'" (52).

As they walked away, the woman began to curse and swear at Jesus. She screamed and cried with rage.

At the next pit they stopped, there was a woman quoting the word of God. She said, "'Jesus is the way, the truth, and the life. No man comes to the Father but by Him. Jesus is the light of the world. Come to Jesus, and He will save you'" (53).

The lost souls nearby reacted in various ways. Some swore and cursed at her. Some told her to stop. Others said, "Is there really hope?" or "Help us, Jesus." Most of all, great cries filled the air (53).

"Jesus knew Mary's thoughts. 'Child, I called this woman at the age of thirty to preach My word and to be a witness of the gospel. I call different ones for different purposes in My body. But if a man or woman, boy or girl doesn't want My Spirit, I will depart'" (54).

The Lord went on to explain that this woman answered the call, grew in the knowledge of the Lord, and learned His voice. She did many good works for Jesus, studied the word of God, prayed often, had many prayers answered, taught people the way of holiness, and was faithful in her house. Until one day, she discovered that her husband was having an affair with another woman. He asked for forgiveness, but this woman his wife "'would not forgive him and try to save their marriage.'

"'But this woman knew My word. She knew to forgive, and she knew that with every temptation there is a way of escape'" (54). She would not forgive him and anger took root. Anger grew inside her. She would not turn it over to Jesus. Over time, she would not pray or read the Bible.

"'She would not listen to Me. Her heart grew bitter, and great sin entered in. Murder grew in her heart where love had once been. And one day, in her anger, she killed her husband and the other woman. Satan then took her over completely, and she killed herself'" (54-55).

"I listened as she responded to Jesus. 'I will forgive now, Lord. Let me out. I will obey You now. See, Lord, I am preaching Your word now. In an hour demons will come to take me to be tormented even worse. For hours they will torture me. Because I was preaching Your word, my torments are worse. Please, Lord, I beg You to let me out'" (56).

In the next pit there was a man crying out to Jesus, "'Lord, help me understand why I am here.'

Jesus answered, 'Peace, be still. You understand why you are here.'

"Jesus turned to Mary and said, 'This man was 23 years old when he came here. He would not listen to My gospel. He heard My word many times and was often in My house. I drew him by My Spirit unto salvation, but he wanted to the world and its lust. He liked to drink and would not heed My call. He was raised in the church, but he would not commit himself to Me. One day he said to Me, 'I will give my life to You one day, Jesus.' But that day never came. One night after a party, he was in a car wreck and was killed. Satan deceived him to the very end' (56).

"'Satan's work is to kill, steal and destroy. If only this young man had listened! It is not the Father's will that any perish. Satan wanted this man's soul, and he destroyed it through carelessness, sin and strong drink. Many homes and lives are destroyed every year because of alcohol'" (57).

The man's cries rang inside Baxter for days. She could not forget the flesh hanging and burning in the flames, the decay, the smell of death, holes where eyes once were, the dirty-gray souls, and the worms that crawled through their bones.

Mary heard a woman's voice crying out in desperation. They arrived at a pit with a woman pleading with Jesus: "'Lord, haven't I been here long enough? My torment is more than I can bear. Please, Lord, let me out!'" Sobs shook her form (58).

"Jesus spoke to her, 'While you were on earth, I called and called for you to come to Me. I pleaded with you to get your heart right with Me, to forgive others, to do right, to stay out of sin. I even visited you in the midnight hour and drew you by My Spirit time after time. With your lips you said you loved Me, but your heart was far from Me. Didn't you know that nothing can be hidden from God? You fooled others, but you could not fool Me. I sent still others to tell you to repent, but you would not listen. You would not hear, you would not see, and in anger you turned them away . . . You were not sorry, nor were you ashamed of what you were doing. You hardened your heart and turned Me away. Now you are lost and forever undone. You have should have listened to Me'" (59-60).

The woman swore and cursed God. Baxter felt the presence of evil spirits and knew that it was they who were cursing and swearing.

"Jesus said, 'The world and all that is in it will pass away, but My words will not pass away'" (60).

The Tunnel of Fear

Jesus and Mary walked on. The pathway was burned, dry, cracked, and barren ground. Jesus walked ahead of Baxter, who followed closely behind Him. Her heart and very spirit were broken from all she had seen and heard.

She looked to her left and right, and there were pits as far as she could see on both sides.

"Jesus said, 'We are now about to enter a tunnel which will take us into the belly of hell. Hell is shaped like a human body lying in the center of the earth. The body is lying on her back, with both arms and both legs stretched out. As I have a body of believers, so hell has a body of sin and death. As the Christ-body is built up daily, so the hell-body is also built up daily'" (63).

As they walked, many called out to Jesus. Others tried to climb out of the pits to reach Him but could not.

Sorrow was always upon Jesus' face as He walked.

The brimstone in the pits reminded Mary of the cookouts in her backyard, where they would have a fire with red hot coals that smoldered for hours.

She was thankful to get to the tunnel, thinking that it could not possibly be as bad as the pits. But how wrong she was!

Baxter first saw great snakes, large rats, and many evil spirits, all running from Jesus. The snakes hissed, and the rats squealed. Vipers and dark shadows were all around. Some of the snakes were as large as four feet around and 25 feet long. Jesus was the only light there.

The sides of the tunnel or cavern were filled with imps and devils. They were going somewhere up and out of the tunnel. Mary found out later that these evil spirits were going out onto the earth to do Satan's work.

"Jesus, feeling her fear, said, 'Fear not; we will be at the end of the tunnel soon. I must show you these things. Come, follow Me' (64).

"'We will soon be to the belly of hell. This part of hell

is seventeen miles high and three miles around like a circle'" (65).

Jesus explained the exact measurements of the belly of hell. To visualize the belly of hell, picture a very large well that is 17 miles high and has a circumference of three miles all the way around the belly.

Mary knew that Jesus was showing her these things so she could warn men and women to avoid hell at all costs.

Activity in Hell

Jesus and Mary came out of the tunnel of fear and stood on a dirty ledge overlooking the belly of hell. Baxter could see a dim, yellow light up ahead and a great amount of activity going on in the belly, also called the center of hell.

"They stopped. Jesus said, 'I am going to take you through the belly of hell, and I am going to reveal many things to you. Come, follow Me.'

"'Ahead are many terrors. They are not the figment of someone's imagination – but they are real. Be sure to tell your readers that demon powers are real. Tell them also that Satan is real, and the powers of darkness are real. But tell them not to despair, for if My people which are called by My name will humble themselves and pray and turn from their wicked ways, then I will hear from heaven and heal their lands and their bodies. Just as surely as heaven is real – even so, hell is also real'" (67-68).

They were in the belly of hell. There was activity ahead, to the right, up a small hill, in a dark corner.

Mary remembered that Jesus told her that it might seem like He would leave her but would not; that He has all power in heaven and in earth; that at times the evil spirits would not know they were there; what they are seeing is real; and that these things will continue to happen until death and hell are cast into the lake of fire (68).

Baxter heard voices and the cries of a soul in torment. She heard cries "you have never thought possible." They were the cries of a man.

"'Listen to Me,' said Jesus. 'What you are about to see and hear is true. Take heed you ministers of the gospel, for these are faithful and true sayings. Awake, evangelists, preachers, and teachers of My word, all of you who are called to preach the gospel of the Lord Jesus Christ. If you are sinning, repent or you will likewise perish'" (69).

They walked up to within 15 feet of the activity. Baxter saw small dark-clothed figures marching around a boxlike object. The box was a coffin, and the figures were demons. It was a real coffin, and there were twelve demons marching around it. They were chanting and laughing. Every demon had a sharp spear in his hand. The demons kept thrusting the spears into the coffin through small openings that lined the outside.

There was a feeling of great fear in the air, and Baxter trembled at the sight before her.

"Jesus knew her thoughts. He said, 'Child, there are many souls in torment here, and there are many different types of torment for these souls. There is greater punishment for those who once preached the gospel and went back into sin, or for those who would not obey the call of God for their lives'" (70).

"Mary heard a desperate cry. 'No hope, no hope!' he called.

They walked up closer to the coffin. A dirty-gray mist filled the inside of the coffin. The demons pushed their spears into the soul of the man inside.

Baxter can never forget the suffering of the man. She begged Jesus to get him out.

"Jesus said: 'My child, peace, be still.' The man saw Jesus.

"'Lord, Lord, let me out. Have mercy.'

"He was a bloody mess. Inside the man was a human heart, and blood spurted from it. The thrusting of the spears was literally piercing his heart.

"'I will serve You now, Lord,' he begged, 'please let me out.'

"'Day and night, he is tormented,' Jesus said, 'He was put here by Satan, and it is Satan who torments him.'

"The man cried, 'Lord, I will now preach the true gospel. I will tell about sin and hell. But please help me out of here' (71).

"Jesus said, 'This man was a preacher of the word of God. There was a time when he serve Me with all his heart and led many people to salvation . . . the lust of the flesh and the deceitfulness of riches led him astray. He let Satan gain the rule over him. He had a big church, a fine car, a large income. He began to steal from the church offerings. He began to teach lies. He spoke mostly half-lies and half-truths. He would not let Me correct him. I sent My messengers to him to tell him to repent and preach the truth, but he loved the pleasures of life more than the life of God. He knew not to teach or preach any other doctrine except the truth as revealed in the Bible. But before he died, he said the Holy Ghost baptism was a lie and that those who claimed to have the Holy Ghost were hypocrites. He said you could be a drunkard and get to heaven, even without repentance. He said God would not send anyone to hell – that God was too good to do that. He caused many good people to fall from the grace of the Lord. He even said that he did not need Me, for he was like a god. He went so far as to hold seminars to teach this false doctrine. He trampled My holy word under his feet. Yet, I continued to love him. My child, it is better to have never known Me than to know Me and turn back from serving Me' (72).

"'He did not listen to Me. When I called he would not hear Me. He loved the easy life. I called and called him to repentance, but he would not come back to Me. One day he was killed and came immediately here. Now Satan torments him for having once preached My word and saved souls for My kingdom. This is his torment.'

"Jesus looked at the man in the coffin with great compassion and said, 'The blood of many lost souls are upon this man's hands. Many of them are in torment here right now.'"

"They continued walking, with sorrowful hearts. As they left, another group of demons arrived. They were about three feet high, dressed in black clothes, with hoods over their faces. There were different shifts of demons tormenting the man" (73).

The Belly of Hell

The next night, they went to hell again.

They first entered into a large open area, filled with lots of activity. The scene was like something from a horror movie. As far as Mary could see, there were souls in torment. The devil and his angels were going about their work. It was semi-dark. Screams of agony and despair pierced the air.

"Jesus said, 'Child, Satan is both the deceiver on earth and the tormentor of souls in hell. Many of the demonic powers seen here also go up to the earth at times to hurt, afflict, and deceive. I am going to show you things that have never before been seen in this much detail . . .' (78).

"'Satan uses many traps and snares to deceive God's people. I will show you many of the cunning and in-sidious tricks of the devil'" (78).

The ground was light brown in color, with no grass or anything living. Everything was dead or dying. Some places were cold and damp. Other areas were hot and dry. Always, there was the putrid, awful stench of burning and decaying flesh mingled with smells of stale garbage, mold, and offal (the waste of a butchered animal).

Up ahead, Mary saw a dark, black object looming ominously. It seemed to move up and down, to con-tract and swell. Every time it moved, it gave off an awful stench – even worse than the normal, horrible smells of hell.

Baxter noticed something like horns, dark in color, coming out of it and going up into the earth. She real-ized it was a large, black heart, with many entrances into it. A dread overcame her.

Jesus knew her thoughts and explained that it was in-deed the heart of hell, that they would later go through it. But they needed to go into the cell block of hell.

The cell block of hell is in a circle in the belly of hell. The cell block area is 17 miles high. The walls are lined with cells, which are like prison cells. They are dug into the dirt walls, with iron bars on the front. The cells are just big enough to hold one person. The cells all have about two feet of dirt between them.

Mary saw a large ditch about six feet deep and won-dered how she would cross it. As soon as she thought that, suddenly they were on a ledge, at the first tier of cells.

The ledge was a walkway around the cells and a van-tage place from which someone could look out over the center of hell.

"Jesus said, 'These things are faithful and true. Death and hell will one day be cast into the lake of fire. Until then, this is hell's holding place. These cells will continue to be here, packed with sinful souls, tormented and suffering.'

"'I gave My life so you would not have to come here. I knew these horrors were real, but My Father's mercy is just as real. If you will let Him, He will forgive you. Call to Him in My name today'" (80).

The Cells in Hell

Jesus and Mary stood on a ledge that was a walkway in front of the first tier of cells. The ledge was about four feet wide. Other ledges and cells were above them, as far as she could see. A giant, massive pit was in the middle of the cell block.

Jesus explained that those in the cell block were in witchcraft or the occult on earth. They were sorcerers, mediums, drug peddlers, idol worshipers, evil people with familiar spirits, witches, and warlocks (male witches). These souls worked the greatest abominations against God. They would not repent. They deceived people and led them away from God.

All around them, Mary could hear the cries, moans, and screams of the damned in the cells. She felt very sick, and great sorrow filled her heart.

"Jesus said: 'I want you to know that Satan comes to steal, kill and destroy. Here in hell there are different torments for different souls. Satan administers this torment until the day of judgment, til death and hell are cast into the lake of fire. Also, a lake of fire comes through hell at times'" (82).

They stopped in front of a cell with an old woman

sitting in a rocking chair. The cell was bare. The walls were of light clay and dirt, molded into the earth. The front door spanned the entire front of the cell and was made of black metal bars with a lock on it. The bars were wide apart. Her color was ashen – flesh mixed with a gray tint. Tears rolled down her cheeks. She was in great pain.

Suddenly, the woman changed forms – first to an old man, then a young woman, then a middle-aged woman, and back to the old lady. She saw Jesus and cried out "'Lord, have mercy on me. Let me out of this place of torment'" (84). She could not reach Him. The changing continued, even her clothes changed.

The woman cried out even stronger, clenching the bars of the door. She cried in terror, as something ripped her flesh from her body. She sat down, now only a skeleton.

Jesus explained the woman was a witch and worshiper of Satan. She also taught people witchcraft. "'Many times, I called on her to repent. She mocked Me and said, "I enjoy serving Satan. I will keep on serving him'" (85).

Satan deceived her into believing she would receive a kingdom of her own as a reward for serving him. He promised she would live forever. When she died and went to hell, Satan laughed in her face and locked her in the cell and torments her day and night.

She taught both white and black witches to do magic. One of her tricks was to change gender/age as she did earlier. She would have fun with it and frighten lesser witches. But now, she suffers the pains of hell, cannot control the changes of gender/age, and her flesh is ripped away with each change. Every so often, she is brought before Satan to be tormented for his pleasure.

Then, a dirty, brown demon with broken wings,

about the size and shape of a large bear, came to the cell and made loud noises. The woman screamed in abject terror as he attacked her and dragged her from the cell.

"'Is there anything we can do?' asked Mary.

"'It's too late, it's too late,' Jesus replied" (87).

The Horrors of Hell

They stopped in front of a cell with a woman, blue-gray in color. Her flesh was dead, and the decayed flesh parts were falling off her bones. Her bones were burned to a deep black, and she wore bits and pieces of ragged clothes. Worms were crawling out of her flesh and bones. A dirty odor filled the cell. She was in a rocking chair and holding a rag doll. Sobs and cries shook her body.

Jesus: "'She was a servant of Satan. She sold her soul to him, and she practiced every kind of evil. Witchcraft is real. This woman taught and practiced witchcraft . . . Those who were teachers of witchcraft received special attention and a greater amount of power from Satan than from those who simply practiced it. She was a soothsayer, a diviner and a medium for her master'" (90).

She held the rag doll tightly. This woman changed forms/ages like the previous woman they saw.

Jesus: "'Just as the true gospel is preached to us by a real minister, so Satan has his counterfeit ministers . . . Satan's evil gifts are like the opposite side of the coin to the spiritual gifts Jesus bestows upon believers. This is the power of darkness. These workers of Satan work in the occult, the witchcraft shops, as palm readers, and in many other ways. A medium of Satan is a powerful Satanic worker . . .' (91).

"'Satan still thinks he can overthrow God and disrupt

God's plan, but he was defeated at the cross. I took the keys away from Satan, and I have all power in heaven and in earth'" (92).

Jesus explained that Satan lied to the woman all along, even after she ended up in hell. In a large black book, Satan saw that the woman won more than 500 souls for him. He continued to torment her. A cackle of evil laughter rang out. Satan stood and pointed a finger at the woman, and a great wind arose and filled the place. A sound like howling thunder rose from him.

Jesus: "'I came to save all men. I desire that all who are lost will repent and call upon My name. It is not My will that any should perish, but have everlasting life. Sad to say, most will not repent of their sins before they die, and they will go to hell. But the way to heaven is the same for all people. You must be born again to enter the kingdom of God. You must come to the Father in My name and repent of your sins. You must sincerely give your heart to God and serve Him'" (94).

Jesus then explained that when the cells are filled, hell enlarges itself to receive more souls.

Also, he explained that if you were blind on earth, you will be blind in hell; if you had one arm on earth, you will have one arm in hell.

As horrible as her descriptions are, Mary saw things in hell that are too horrible to tell. She writes: "I saw things in hell that are too horrible to tell . . . I also saw things that God would not let me write" (95).

Jesus explained that though torments are different for different souls, all are burned with fire.

Jesus told her about the place called the "fun center," shaped like a circus arena. Those who knowingly served Satan are brought to this place. They were leaders in the occult. They deceived many and caused others to follow Satan. Several souls are brought to the center ring to be the entertainment. Those who were deceived by these occult leaders torture those in the ring. In one such torture, a soul's bones were torn apart and buried in different parts of hell. The soul felt tremendous pain.

Jesus: "'I took the keys of hell away from Satan many years ago. I came and opened these cells and let My people out . . .'" (97).

Suddenly they were about a half-mile up in the air, in the center of the belly of hell. All at once, a hurricane-force wind and mighty rushing sound came near them. Waves of fire rushed up the walls, burning all in its path. The flames went into every cell. Mary heard an evil sound. She looked, and Satan was standing with his back to them. He was all aflame. He was not burned though. He actually caused the fire. As he moved his arms, great balls of fire shot from him.

Cries and screams came from the cells. The demons joined in the laughter.

Jesus: "'Satan feeds on evil. He glories in pain and suffering and gains power from it'" (99).

A reddish-yellow flame with brown edges grew around Satan. A wild and gusty wind blew his garments which did not burn. He ascended in a cloud of smoke. With a loud voice, he announced that unless all those souls worshiped him, he would give them a turn in the fun circle.

Jesus explained that all those in the cell block heard the true gospel while on earth, and that many times His Spirit drew them, but they would not give attention to or listen or come to Jesus to be saved.

"'My salvation is free. Whoever will, let him come and be saved from this place of everlasting punishment. I will not cast him out . . . even if you have a written agreement with the devil, My power will break it, and My shed blood will save you'" (101).

The Heart of Hell

At night, they went back to hell. They walked along the belly. It was the same rotting flesh, the odor of evil, the stale, hot air everywhere. Jesus knew Mary's thoughts: "'I'll never leave you or forsake you. I know you are weary, but I will strengthen you'" (103).

His touch did strengthen her, and they continued on. Ahead Mary saw a large black object, almost as big as a baseball field. It was moving up and down. It was the heart of hell.

Large arms or horns came out of the heart. They went up and out of hell into the earth and over the earth (see Diagram of Hell, pages 20-21). Around the heart, the earth was dry and brown. For about 30 feet in all directions next to the heart, the earth was burned and dried to a rusty, brown color.

The heart was the blackest of blacks. There was also another color like the scales of a snake's skin intermixed with the black.

Mary wondered what the heart's purpose could be.

Jesus: "'These branches, which look like arteries of a heart, are pipelines that go up through the earth to spill out evil upon it. These are the horns that Daniel saw, and they represent evil kingdoms on the earth. Some have already been, some shall be, and some are now. Evil kingdoms will arise, and the Antichrist will rule over many people, places, and things. If possible, the very elect will be deceived by him. Many will turn away and worship the beast and his image.'

"'Out of these main branches or horns, smaller branches will grow. Out of the smaller branches will come demons, evil spirits and all manner of evil forces.

They will be released upon the earth and instructed by Satan to do many evil works. These kingdoms and evil forces will obey the beast, and many will follow him to destruction. It is here in the heart of hell that these things begin'" (105).

Jesus instructed Mary to write these words and to tell them to the world.

Jesus asked her to follow Him, and they walked up stairs into the heart. It was total darkness, and Mary could barely breathe.

Suddenly, Jesus was gone! It was unthinkable. She was alone in the heart of hell. Horror took hold of her. Fear gripped her soul. Death took hold of her.

She cried out to Jesus. She called and called, but no one answered. She started to run. As she touched the walls, they seemed to breathe and move.

Then she realized beings were near her. She heard the sound of laughter as two demons grabbed both her hands. A dim light was around them. They put chains on her arms and dragged her deeper into the heart. She screamed for Jesus but no answer. She fought with all her might, but they dragged her on as if she offered no resistance at all.

A force rubbed her body, causing horrible pain. It felt like her flesh was being ripped off her body. They threw her into a cell and locked the door. They laughed sarcastically and told her that her cries would do no good; that she would be taken before their master so he could torment her.

After a while, she began to feel the side of the wall. It was round and soft like something alive. Fear – the most awesome fear – gripped her soul. Mary realized she was lost forever with no hope at all. She sobbed and cried out to Jesus over and over again.

As a dim light appeared, she could see other cells.

Inside all the cells, a kind of muddy, gooey substance flowed. A woman's voice from the next cell said, "'You are lost in this place of torment. There is no way out of here.'" She was awake, but the occupants of the other cells seemed to be in a trance. "'No hope!'" the woman cried (108).

The woman told Mary that those in the heart are not tormented as bad as other people; but later, Mary found out the woman was lying. The woman also said that those in the heart are sometimes brought before Satan, who tortures them for his pleasure, feeding and growing strong on their cries of despair and sorrow. The woman was a prostitute on earth.

The two demons came back to Mary's cell and forced her along a rough pathway. Their touch was like a burning flame. A roaring fire sprang up in front of her. It felt like her flesh was being ripped off her body. The most excruciating pain she has ever felt swept over her. Evil spirits in the form of bats were biting her all over.

Mary was pushed and pulled until she came to a wide open place and was thrown before a dirty type of altar. On the altar, there was a large, open book. She heard evil laughter and recognized she was lying in the dirt before Satan.

He said: "'I waited for you for a long time, and at last I have you. You tried to escape me, but now I have you'" (110). Fear came over her. Her flesh was torn from her. A large chain was wrapped around her body. She looked at her body: it was a skeleton full of dead men's bones. Worms crawled inside of her, and a fire began at her feet and enveloped her in flames (111).

She cried out for Jesus. "The devil said: 'There is no Jesus here. I am your king now. You will be with me here forever. You are mine now'"(111).

Mary could feel with the keenest of senses, fear, hatred, excruciating pain, and sorrow beyond measure.

Satan said, "'I am your Lord now,'" and called for a demon, who arrived quickly. The evil spirit had a large body, a face like a bat, claws for hands, and an evil odor. It grabbed Mary. Another demon with hair and a face like a boar also grabbed her.

Satan: "'Take her to the deepest part of the heart – a place where horrors are ever before her eyes. There she will learn to call me Lord'" (112).

They took her to a dark, dark place and threw her into something cold and clammy. It was cold and burning at the same time.

All at once a light filled the place. Jesus appeared and took her into His arms. Instantly she was back at home.

"Tenderly Jesus spoke and said, 'My child, hell is real. But you could never know for sure until you had experienced it for yourself. Now you know the truth and what it is really like to be lost in hell. Now you can tell others about it. I had to let you go through that so you would know without a doubt'" (112-113).

Mary was so sad and so tired. She collapsed in Jesus' arms. He restored her whole, but she wanted to go far, far away – from everyone, even from Jesus.

For days, she was very sick. It was many days before she was fully recovered.

Outer Darkness

They returned to hell night after night. When they were near the heart, enormous fear gripped Mary's soul. Only through the mercies of God could she continue.

One night, they stopped before a group of demons, who were singing, chanting, and praising Satan. They said, "'We will go to this house today and torment those that are there. We will get more power from Lord Satan if we do this right. We will cause a lot of pain, sickness, and grief to them all'" (115). They danced and sang evil songs to Satan.

One said, "'We will have to watch very carefully for those who believe in Jesus, for they can cast us out.'

"'We are not going to those who know Jesus and the power of His name.'"

Jesus: "'My angels keep My people from these evil spirits, and their works do not prosper. I also protect many of the unsaved, even though they do not know it'" (116)

Jesus exhorted Mary about the importance of the gospel being preached. He said "'the truth will set men free, and I will protect them from evil. In My name there is deliverance and freedom. I have all power in heaven and earth. Do not fear Satan, but fear God'" (116).

They came upon a very large and dark man, actually an angel, about 30 feet tall. He was holding something like a large disk in his hand. Jesus: "'This place is called outer darkness'" (117).

The angel was turning slowly, holding the disk high up in the air. There was a fire in the middle of the disk and blackness on the outer edge. The angel held the disk in his hand and reached far back in order to get more leverage.

Jesus: "Remember My word says, 'The children of the kingdom shall be cast into outer darkness.'"

Mary: "'You mean your servants are here?'"

Jesus: "'Yes, servants that turned back after I called them. Servants who loved the world more than Me and went back to wallowing in the mire of sin. Servants that would not stand for truth and holiness. It is better that one never starts than to turn back after beginning to serve Me' (117-118).

"The angel cast the large disk far, far out into the darkness.

"'My word means just what it says: they "shall be cast into outer darkness"'" (118).

Jesus and Mary were in the air following the disk through space. In the fire in the center of the disk, people were swimming in and out, over and under the flaming waves. No demons, only souls burning in a sea of fire.

Outside the disk was the blackest of darkness. People were trying to swim to the edges of the disk. Some would almost reach the sides when a suction force from inside the disk would drag them back into the flames. Their forms would turn to skeletons with misty-gray souls. Mary knew this was another part of hell.

The Center of Hell

Mary's visits to hell with Jesus were almost completed. One night, Jesus said: "'My child, for this purpose you were born, to write and tell what I have told you and shown you. For these things are faithful and true. I have called you forth to tell the world through you that there is a hell, but I have made a way of escape. I will not show you all parts of hell. And there are hidden things which I cannot reveal to you. But I will show you much . . .'" (147).

They went to the belly of hell again. They were on a ledge beside a cell. They stopped in front of a cell with a beautiful woman. The letters "B.C." were over the top of the cell.

"'Lord, I knew you would come someday. Please let me out of this place of torment,' said the woman, who was wearing clothes of an ancient era. She began to pull at the bars and cry.

"Softly Jesus said, 'Peace, be still.' He spoke to her with sadness in His voice. 'Woman, you know why you are here.'

"'Yes, but I can change. I remember when you let all those others out of paradise. I remember Your words of salvation. I will be good now,' she cried, 'and I will serve you.' She clenched the bars with her tiny fists and screamed, 'Let me out! Let me out!'" (148).

Then she began to change. Her clothing burned. Her flesh fell off, and all that remained was a black skeleton with burned-out holes for eyes and a hollow shell of a soul. Mary watched in horror as the old woman fell to the floor.

On earth, the woman was a soothsayer and a witch. She taught the art of witchcraft.

Jesus: "'Satan uses many devices to destroy good men and women. He works day and night, trying to get people to serve him. If you fail to choose to serve God, you have chosen to serve the devil. Choose life, and the truth will set you free'" (149)

They stopped in front of a cell with a man calling out "'Who is there? Who is there?'" Mary wondered why he was calling out.

Jesus: "'He is blind.'" The man was in the cell, with his back to Jesus. He was a skeleton form with fire and the smell of death on him. He was flailing the air and crying, "'Help me! Help, someone!'"

"Tenderly, Jesus said, 'Man, peace, be still.'

"The man turned, 'Lord, I knew you would come for me. I repent now. Please let me out. I know I was a horrible person and used my handicap for selfish gain. I know I was a sorcerer and deceived many for Satan. But Lord, I repent now. Please let me out. Day and night I am tormented in these flames, there is no water.

I am so thirsty. Won't you give me a drink of water?'

"Jesus said, 'All sorcerers and workers of evil will have their part in the lake which burns with fire and brimstone, which is the second death'" (150).

They came to a cell with a man who was a skeleton, full of flames and worms. Jesus explained that the man was a disciple of Satan, a liar who deceived many. He made fun of Jesus' salvation and the Holy Spirit. As Jesus and Mary walked away, the man began to curse and say many evil things against the Lord.

Jesus: "'Whoever will may come to Me, and he that loses His life for My sake shall find it, and that more abundantly. But sinners must repent while still alive on earth. It is too late to repent when they arrive here. Many sinners want to serve God and Satan, or they believe they have unlimited time to accept the grace God offers. The truly wise will choose this day whom they will serve'" (151).

The next cell they visited had a man who was huddled on the floor. His bones were black from burning. His soul was a dirty-gray mist inside. Parts of his body were missing. Smoke and flames came up around him. Worms crawled inside of him.

Jesus explained that the man was a murderer and had hate in his heart. He did not believe that God would forgive him. He refused the gospel, though he was given many opportunities to serve God and believe the gospel.

Mary was so sad she was almost sick. They came to a cell with a woman. She cried out, "'Help me.'" She had real eyes, not burned-out sockets.

"'Lord, I will do what is right now. I once knew you, and you were my Savior'" (153). Her hands clenched the bars of the cell. Big pieces of burning flesh fell from her, and only bones were left.

The woman explained that Jesus healed her of cancer and told her to sin no more. She tried and tried to witness for Jesus, but realized it was not popular. She went back into the world, and the lust of the flesh devoured her. Nightclubs and strong drink became more important than Jesus. Later she did not realize she was possessed by Satan. She kept thinking, I still have time. Tomorrow I will turn back to Jesus. She waited too long, and now it is too late.

Then they visited a cell with a man who confessed his failings. He thought about making Jesus Lord of his life, but he did not want to walk the straight and narrow way. He wanted the broad way and sin, which was easier. He desired strong drink and the world more than obedience.

"'For years I have been tormented in this place. I know what I am, and I know I will never get out. I am tormented day and night in these flames and these worms. I cry, but no one comes to help. No one cares for my soul – no one cares for soul.' He fell into a heap and continued to cry" (156).

They walked on. They came to a cell with a woman picking worms off her bones. She began to cry when she saw Jesus. "'Help me, Lord,' she said, 'I will be good. Please let me out.' She arose and clenched the bars. As she cried, sobs shook her body.

She said, "On earth, I worshiped the Hindu gods and many idols. I would not believe the gospel the missionaries preached to me, though I heard it many times. One day I died. I cried for my gods to save me from hell, but they could not. Now, Lord, I'd like to repent.'"

"Jesus said, 'It's too late'" (156).

List of lost souls in *A Divine Revelation of Hell*

Pits:

1. Woman – no eyes, no hair, crying out, "Lord, lord, I want out of here!" (24)

2. Man who had been in hell for 40 years. People showed him the way, and he heard gospel on earth, but he mocked Jesus. He asked Jesus if he could go warn his people to repent while on earth (26).

3. Woman, 80 years old, one leg from cancer. She knew Jesus at one time but turned her back on Jesus and cursed Him. Even after she turned her back on Jesus, He still tried to draw her by His Spirit (28).

4. Woman who was beautiful and found riches, fame, and fortune. Jesus called and called her to Himself, but she refused. Over time she served Satan more and more. She died in a car wreck (31).

5. Man who was a minister and preached the gospel but had sins and wrongs summarized (41).

6. Woman. She had sinful affairs with many men and caused homes to be broken apart. Jesus still loved her and offered her salvation (44-46).

7. Woman who went to church but led double life (50).

8. Woman who served the Lord on earth, learned His voice, did many good works for Jesus, taught people the way of holiness. Her husband had an affair with another woman. The woman, his wife, would not forgive him, and anger took root. Over time she became bitter and one day, she murdered her husband and the woman and killed herself. Because she served the Lord, in hell her torments are worse (52-56).

9. Man who was raised in church but did not commit himself to the Lord. He preferred the world and its lust

and strong drink. He died at age 23 in a car wreck (56).

10. Woman who on earth said she loved Jesus, but her heart was far from Him. She fooled others on earth but did not repent (59).

11. Man who was a preacher on earth. He was led astray by the lust of the flesh and the deceitfulness of riches. He stole money from his church's offerings. He taught false doctrine, half-lies, and half-truths. He would not repent (69).

Cells:

11. Old woman who changes gender and age. She was a witch and worshiper of Satan on earth. (83).

12. Woman in a cell in the heart of hell (108).

13. Woman of an ancient era. "B.C." was above her cell. On earth, she was a soothsayer, witch, and teacher of witchcraft. She remembered when Jesus let souls out of paradise (147).

14. Blind man, a sorcerer while on earth. He used his handicap for selfish gain (150).

15. Man, a disciple of Satan and a liar. On earth, he made fun of Jesus' salvation and the Holy Spirit (151).

16. Man, a murderer with hate in his heart (152).

17. Woman who was healed of cancer. She tried to witness for Jesus but went back into sin and was eventually possessed by Satan. She did not repent (154).

18. Man, in rebellion, desired strong drink and the world more than obeying God's commands (155).

19. Woman, a Hindu on earth. Her gods could not save her from hell (156).

TWO

Kenneth Hagin

Kenneth Hagin (1917-2003) was a minister and founder of the Word of Faith charismatic denomination, which today has more than 180 churches in 46 nations.

Hagin was a longtime influential Pentecostal preacher, teacher, writer, and leader, based in Tulsa, Oklahoma, USA. During his more than 50 years of ministry, his ministry published more than 65 million of his books and booklets. Hagin was originally from McKinney, Texas, a suburb of Dallas. His son Kenneth Hagin, Jr., now leads the Rhema and Word of Faith Ministries.

Hagin, Sr., was known for having numerous visions of, visitations from, and experiences with Jesus Christ.

Kenneth was born prematurely with a deformed heart. Doctors did not expect him to live long. He did live, but he was not able to do normal childhood activities such as running, playing, and the like.

In 1933, when Kenneth was 15 years old, he was bed-fast for five months. Several doctors said he would likely die. On a particular night, he had taken a turn for the worse, and his family and grandparents were in the room with him. His heart stopped beating.

As fast a snap of a finger, his blood ceased to circulate. He leaped out of his body. Hagin did not lose consciousness; he jumped out of his body like a diver would leap off a diving board into a swimming pool.

Kenneth knew he was out of his body and could see him family.

He began to descend – down, down, into a pit, like going down into a well, cavern, or cave.

Kenneth actually tried to say "good-bye." Later, his family told him that his "good-bye" sounded like it came from way down in a cave or cavern.

He went down feet first – down, down, down, down. He could look up and see the lights of the earth. The lights finally faded away. Darkness encompassed around him. The darkness was blacker than any night he had ever seen.

The farther down he went, the darker it became. Until finally, he could see flickers of light on the wall of darkness. He came to the bottom of the pit.

Many years later, his experience seemed as if it had happened just recently.

Hagin noticed what was causing the light. Out in front of him, beyond the gates or the entrance to hell, he saw giant, great orange flames with a white crest.

He was pulled toward hell just like a magnet pulls metal into itself. He knew that once he had entered through those gates, he could not come back.

Kenneth tried to slow down his descent, because when he came to the bottom of the pit, there was still a slant downward.

He was conscious of some kind of creature that met him at the pit's bottom. He didn't look at him. Ken's gaze was fixed on the gates, though he knew a creature was beside him.

The creature took Hagin by the arm to escort him in. While this was happening, away above the blackness and the darkness, a voice spoke. It sounded like a male voice, but he didn't know if it was God, Jesus, an angel, or who. The voice was not speaking English but rather a foreign language.

The place shook at the few words he spoke! The creature took his hand off Ken's arm. There was a power like a suction to Hagin's back parts that pulled him up. He floated away from the entrance to hell until he stood in the shadows. Then, like a suction from above, he floated up, headfirst, through the darkness.

Before he got to the top, he could see the light. It was like being way down in a well and seeing the light up above.

Ken came up to his grandpa's house, onto the porch. He could see the porch swing and the giant cedar trees in the yard. He stood on the porch for a second and then went right through the wall! Then he seemed to leap into his body like a man would slip his foot inside his boot in the morning.

He had seen his grandmother sitting on the edge of the bed, holding him in her arms.

When he entered his body, he spoke to her. Kenneth knew he might slip again into death, so he asked to say good-bye to his mother. She was outside praying. He thanked his mother and also his grandmother for all they had done for him.

Then he died again. He felt his blood cease to circulate. He began to go down, down, down, down, until the darkness encompassed him. The light faded away.

The farther down he went, the hotter and darker it became. He came to the bottom of the pit and saw the entrance to hell, or the gates. He was conscious that the same creature met him.

Hagin felt like he was being pulled down. But he tried to slow down his descent. The creature took hold of his arm again. And again, a voice spoke which shook the place. It was a man's voice in a foreign tongue. Again, Kenneth felt a suction on his back and floated up to the shadows of darkness. Then he was pulled up headfirst back to earth. He entered his body.

He began to talk to his grandmother again. Kenneth asked to say good-bye to his Granddad. He was not there, so he thanked his grandmother for all his grand-dad had done for him.

Ken asked about his siblings. Then his heart stopped for a third time.

He began to descend again. This time, he was really scared that he might not come back to earth.

Darkness descended upon him. In the darkness, he cried out, "God! I belong to the church! I've been baptized in water!"

There was no answer. He said it again. He waited. There was no answer. So he screamed it a third time.

He came to the bottom of the pit. He could feel the heat beating him on the face. He approached the entrance, the gates of hell.

He heard the voice again. The place shook and trembled. He started to go up again.

As he was going up, he began to pray. His spirit man began to pray: "O God! I come to You in the Name of the Lord Jesus Christ! I ask You to forgive me of my sins and to cleanse me from all sin" (15).

Kenneth would go on to be healed and do the work God called him to do.

THREE

Michael Yeager

Michael Yeager grew up in Chicago, Illinois, USA. He has been a pastor now for more than 30 years.

As a young boy, he faced many health issues. At age 15, he dropped out of school and joined a gang. In the military, his alcohol and drug problems became worse.

In the Navy, while stationed in Alaska, one night he felt a strong urge to pray. A frightening darkness enveloped him. He felt an earthquake. The floor rippled like waves of the sea. The floor ripped open. A hole emerged. Michael began to fall into it, screaming and yelling for help. He tried to hold on but continued falling in the pit.

In fear, he tried to stop his fall. He could feel, touch, smell, hear, and see everything going on. In fact, everything was amplified beyond his normal senses.

A violent and overwhelming hot wind was blowing up from the hole, into his face. It was suffocating, nauseating, and stinking. It smelled like rotten eggs and sulfur. It made it almost impossible to breathe.

The hole seemed to be bottomless. Finally he was out of the hole, out of the tunnel. He entered into a gigantic, endless cavern. He was high, high above an ocean of liquefied, swirling, and blazing fire.

Below him was a frightening, boiling lake of fire. It was burning, churning, and bubbling. The lake seemed to have an aggressive, living fury. Fire and brimstone were exploding, sending flames rising thousands of feet in the air. There were air-shattering explosions, like volcanoes erupting. It glowed red, orange, and yellow.

It was like it pulsated and radiated similar to hot charcoal in a furnace, with molten steel, liquefied stone, and swirling gases.

Though he felt like he was 10,000 feet above the lake, the heat from it was so intense that his very flesh felt as if it was withering, melting, and burning. It felt like his flesh was being ripped off his body.

His skin began to burn, as did his clothes and hair. He screamed like a madman. His lungs felt like they were burning.

As he was falling, he began to hear an eerie sound, like a humming sound – a throbbing, deep, continual moan. As he continued to fall, the sound increased in its intensity, becoming an ear-piercing, overwhelming, never-ending sound. He wondered, "what could be causing such terrible, heart-wrenching, horror-filled sounds?"

He realized the sounds were from human beings. They were screaming, wailing, groaning, and moaning with an incredible, intense, overwhelming pain, in agony and torment.

His whole body began to shake violently.

About 2,000 feet from the lake, Michael faced unbearable, unbelievable all-consuming pain. His body felt like it was on fire. Yet, he was fully aware of everything transpiring around him. If anything, his five senses were more alive than ever before.

He could see on the lake's surface little black objects bobbing up and down like fishing corks.

Yeager writes: "I am not embellishing in the least. If anything, I find myself at a loss to fully express what hell is really like . . . it was more real than the flesh and blood world I live in . . . my experience was both physical and literal. It was not a vision or a dream. I could touch, taste, see, smell, and hear all that transpired. My five senses and my emotional, mental, and psychological perceptions were even more alive in the encounter than they are now."

Then, he was out of hell. It was as if hell vomited him out. He felt like he was shot out of a cannon. He found himself standing on the edge of a high and steep cliff. He was looking straight down into the ocean of torment he had just been suffering in.

He must have been more than 1,000 feet high above the boiling fire. Looking around, he saw flat land with no vegetation. The soil was brownish gray, with rocks and boulders. On the horizon, he saw a mountain range. In the distance, there was a wide, dark, slow-flowing river. Like a massive waterfall, it was pouring its contents over the edge of the cliff, into the mouth of hell.

Yeager feared the river. He wanted to run as far away as possible from it. He sensed it would bring him tremendous pain. But the Holy Spirit was prompting him to go investigate the river.

When he got there, he realized it was not full of water. It was full of people – multitudes and multitudes of people. Yeager could see that the people were of all nations, tongues, and people; a range of ages, from young to old; and all professions. He did not see any infants or little children in the masses (Revelation 17:15, Joel 3:14, Isaiah 11:6-9, John 1:9).

As far as Yeager could see in the distance and horizon, the multitudes of people were packed onto a wide, asphalt road. He could see their faces: they did not seemed concerned at all about where they were headed. They were laughing and talking, etc. As they got close to the mouth of hell, they would wake up and realize where they were headed. At the very edge, they would lose their mind in terror and fear (Mark 4:19, Luke 12:16-21, 1 Thessalonians 5:3, Matthew 24:37-39).

As they began to fall over the cliff, they would try with all their might to keep from falling. They would dig their fingers into the surface, clawing at the rough cliff walls to try to save themselves. The cliff was covered and matted with human blood, flesh, and bones. Yeager could hear their pitiful screams as they tried to stop their descent into hell. He could see them spinning and tumbling head over heals into the abyss. It was horrifying.

Even worse, hell is enlarging itself to receive all these souls (Isaiah 5:14, Proverbs 27:20a).

God Himself is heartbroken about people ending up in hell (Isaiah 63:9a, Hebrews 4:15).

FOUR

Curtis "Earthquake" Kelley

Curtis "Earthquake" Kelley is a Pastor and Evangelist based in Los Angeles, California, USA. Kelley experienced hell when he was 15 years old. He ministers worldwide and shares his unique testimony.

Kelley is one of 11 children in a family from Stamford, Connecticut, just 30 miles from Manhattan, New York City. His family has a history of practicing black arts, including voodoo and witchcraft. Young Curtis grew up using and dealing drugs, running with gangs, and practicing the black arts. As a young man, he was a professional boxer, earning the nickname Earthquake for his ferocious punching.

God took him to hell in the early 1970s.

With a few friends, Earthquake had taken four different drugs and passed out. The spirits he knew of grabbed him and began dragging him down into a pit.

After he landed, there were many demons tormenting him, hitting him with things, in his mouth and eyes, beating him up. They told him that he worked for them, that it was all a trap and now he was in hell.

In hell, Kelley could hear peoples' cries of torment and feel the heat of hell. Hell was loud and had a nauseating, stinking smell.

Later, Kelley realized that those drugs were a trap and trick to cause his heart to stop, so that he would die and end up in hell for eternity.

"'Hell is a real place, for sure. It's a nasty, horrible, ugly, stinking, sulfur-smelling place. You can't even hardly describe it. It is 24 hours a day of nothing but torment and misery. You hear all kinds of noise and promises and terrible things.'"

Suddenly some hands of light reached down, grabbed his shoulders, and began pulling him out of the pit. The demons held on to him and screamed that he was theirs.

Kelley came back to earth. He heard God tell him: "You were saved because of your mother's prayers and because we have a work for you to do."

FIVE

Ron Reagan

Ronald Reagan is an evangelist and pastor who as a young man had a vision of hell.

Reagan along with his wife ministers and preaches the gospel of Jesus Christ around the world. His ministry is Reagan Ministries. Ronald is originally from east Tennessee, USA.

In the early 1970s, Reagan was in his early 20s, married with children, but his family was broken and suffering. He himself was involved in drugs and criminal activity, as he had been since his youth.

In 1972, he had a near death experience after being severely injured in a fight. It was then that he saw a vision of hell. He was in an ambulance when the vision began.

"It appeared as if the ambulance exploded in flames. Immediately I was moving through that smoke as if through a tunnel. After some period of time, coming out of the smoke and out of the darkness, I began to hear the voices of a multitude of people screaming, and moaning, and crying. As I looked down, the sensation was of looking down on a volcanic opening, and seeing the fire, and smoke and people inside this burning place. They were screaming and crying. They were burning, but they weren't burning up, they weren't being consumed. And then the sensation of moving downward into this.

Reagan's wife was with him at the time. She recalls: "He was thrashing about, and moaning and groaning. It was like there was a battle going on. It was scary to me that I could feel it. It was like light and darkness. It was like he was fighting against something. I didn't know what. But now I know, he was seeing the vision of hell."

Reagan: "The most terrible part of it, was that I began to recognize many of the people I was seeing in these flames, as if a close-up lens of a camera was bringing their faces close to me. I could see their features, and their agony and pain and frustration. And a number of them began to call my name, and said, 'Ronnie, don't come to this place. There's no way out. There's no escape. If you come here, there's no way out.'

"And I looked into the face of one who had died in a robbery attempt, who had been shot to death and bled to death. And I looked into the face of two others who had been drunk and died in an automobile accident. And I looked into the face of others who died of drug overdoses, and the agony and pain. I believe the most painful part of it was the loneliness. The depression was so heavy, that there was no hope, no way out of this place. The smell was like sulfur, like an electric welder. The stench was terrible.

"I had seen people killed. I had done time in prison for manslaughter myself. I grew up in a reform school and a jail cell. I was beat on mercifully as a child by a father who had temper problems and alcohol problems. I was a runaway at age 12. I felt like there was nothing in this world that could frighten me. My life was wrecked, my marriage was wrecked, my health was wrecked. But now I am seeing something that literally scares me to death. Because I don't understand it. As I'm looking into this pit, this place of fire and screams and torment, I just fade out into blackness. When I opened my eyes, I'm in a hospital room in Knoxville, TN. My wife is by my side. There have been multiple stitches put in my body, almost 100 stitches. My arm was spared. All I could visualize was what had just happened.

"I could still hear the screams. I could still smell the terrible smell. I could still feel the heat. I could still hear the voices of people that I had known through the years. In the days to come, I tried every way to get that out of my mind. I tried to get drunk, I could not get drunk. I tried to get stoned, I could not get stoned. I tried everything that I could to get this off my mind, and I could not. One morning, several months later, I came home, walked in the house, and to my room, and my wife was sitting up reading. She said, 'Ronnie, tonight I accepted the Lord Jesus Christ as my savior.'

"Our life had been filled with agony. She grew up in Chicago, her father was a bartender on the south side, she knew nothing about the Bible or church. I had put wrinkles in her face through my abuse, violence, and alcoholism, drug addiction, being gone months at a time. She said, 'Jesus saved me tonight. Would you go with me tonight to hear about this man Jesus.' I agreed to go with her. Two weeks later, November 2, 1972, I found Jesus Christ."

SIX

Carmelo Brenes

Carmelo Brenes is a pastor and evangelist.

In 1982, during a near death experience (NDE), he visited hell.

He felt everything go dark and began walking through a dark tunnel. He could hear moans and screams. The fear in him was increasing more and more. The tunnel was cold and dark. He began to see gigantic snakes.

All the people there were crying out for water. They came to a large plateau with many different chambers and divisions that contained different people.

Terror invaded Brenes' soul. His whole life was passing before his eyes. He shouted, "Have mercy on me my Lord! . . . I beg you to help me! Help me Lord!"

Brenes heard a voice say, "Stop! I am not the God of adulterers, I am not the God of fornicators, I am not the God of liars. Why do you call me Lord, if I am not a God of those who boast and are proud? Come and I will show you the things going on in this place that is waiting for all who have not been willing to follow My way and have walked after the imaginations of their own hearts."

They came to a cell which had a woman in a rocking chair. Her body was transformed because she was a witch. She screamed with groans and moans. She asked for help because her whole being was burning in flames.

The Lord spoke, "The wages of sin is death, and those who arrive in this place will never get out again."

The Lord showed him places down in the earth, like openings in the earth, that had some kind of burning oil where there were beings burning in flames. When the people tried to get out, a demon came at once to put them inside that place again.

There were people who had once been part of Christian churches but were in hell, begging for mercy. Once a man is dead, mercy cannot be reached anymore.

The Lord says in His word: "And as it is appointed for men to die once, but after this the judgment . . ." (Hebrews 9:27).

Jesus took Brenes to a place where there were pastors, evangelists, missionaries, and many believers who were in hell for various reasons.

There was a missionary who opened a mission in Africa but took half of the money intended for the mission.

There were ministers and servants of God who had robbed tithes and offerings from their churches.

Brenes writes: "At death, the real life begins, and the real personality of the believer or the sinner shows up and begins to live; either in the glory of God or in condemnation and eternal shame. That choice, you make it today and now; right at this moment is when you can think over and meditate on where you want to spend your eternity . . ."

They arrived at a place with demons of all types, shapes, and forms. Some of them had one arm, one eye, and one leg. The Lord said these were demons of destruction.

The torment in that location is "so terrible that the souls cannot stop and remember all the things that they did while on earth."

Just like the rich man in the Parable of the Rich Man and Lazarus, people in hell remember their life on earth.

If children can distinguish between good and evil and are not in the ways of the Lord, even they can end up in hell. Nothing is hidden from the eyes of the Lord.

Brenes saw and encountered people who believed they were holy on earth but were now in hell, begging for mercy and another chance. Carmelo's soul ached for them with an intense pain.

He saw a woman who was actually preaching the word of God while in hell. She read John 3:16 out loud. Brenes asked Jesus why she was there. Jesus explained that the woman "could never forgive her husband." (See Matthew 6:14-15).

Brenes saw people burning in flames, with bodies that were a dark gray color. They moaned and shouted in pain and terror. Their flesh melted and fell from their bodies. Their skin fell from their bodies until they were just dark gray bones.

Worms continually attacked those in hell, crawling in and eating their flesh and even their bones.

SEVEN

Mario Martinez

Mario Martinez is a prophet and follower of Jesus Christ. As a young man, he had an experience in hell. Since then, he has been in ministry in California, Nevada, and Kansas, USA, where he is based now.

Martinez had a rough childhood and youth in east Los Angeles, California, USA. His father was very abusive physically and emotionally to Mario, his two siblings, and his mother. After fighting with his father, Mario's dad kicked his young son out of the home. Mario joined gangs and eventually ended up in prison for seven years.

After his time in prison, one night in the late 1990s Mario felt an urge to stay home and not join friends on evening. When he fell asleep, suddenly he noticed that he was out of his body. He was actually above his body looking down at himself.

He started spinning faster and faster. He heard demons laughing at him. After a loud noise, he found himself in a pitch black dark place. There were dead trees around. The sandy ground was a grayish dirty color. Something behind him made a light that allowed him to see what was around him.

He heard a noise around him. He saw a big dark tunnel and started moving toward it. Mario saw a distant light at the end of the tunnel. Though he was moving, he was not walking. He was floating into this tunnel, with arms stretched out.

His hands were getting so heavy they were hurting him. There were shackles with balls and chains on his hands.

There were five demons around him, dressed in black; two in front, two beside him on each side, and one in the back. The demons all looked grotesque and wicked. Some looked like rats with long noses and faces, while others looked like bats. Their eyes had a very evil, wicked look and were different colors, such as yellow, red, orange, or green.

Martinez knew that these demons wanted to destroy him and any soul. They were full of hatred. As he kept moving forward toward the end of the tunnel, he yelled, "Where am I?" The demons did not answer but instead kept hideously laughing and snickering as they escorted him forward. The tunnel was slimy and dirty.

Mario started to smell a horrible smell. It was so terrible he wanted to die. He could not die, though: he was already dead and out of his body. The smell was burning flesh.

As he got to the end of the tunnel, the small light was gone. Another light appeared. Suddenly, a great fire "opened up" like the light a person in a dark room sees when they open the curtains to the sunshine.

A voice said, "Walk into it." As he did, he was on the

other side, where there were demons, fire, and many people screaming and shouting. People were being burned in the fire. Mario could feel the fear, anger, and hatred. There was no love. There were rivers with skeletons in them.

Suddenly, he saw a big angel on his right side. The angel was smiling and holding a sword of fire in his hand.

The angel said, "Mario, look at me!" Mario was so scared that he was not looking at the angel. The angel asked him, "Do you know where you are?" Mario replied: "No."

"If this was your day, this would be your portion," said the angel. "This is where you would spend your eternal life. Who is your god?"

Mario replied: "I don't know." Mario saw a small window open, with a vision of two men named Ronny and Donny who visited and befriended Mario and other boys in his neighborhood, telling them about Jesus. Mario was eight years old when he asked Jesus into his life but later did not walk with Him.

The angel repeated, "Who is your God?" Mario replied: "Jesus." The angel said, "Scream the name of your God!" Mario screamed: "Jesus!" The name "Jesus" echoed through the tunnel and where he had been. Then, WHAM! Mario was back in his body on earth.

He gasped for air. Mario then got on his knees, raised his arms and hands, and ask God for forgiveness and to be his Lord and Savior.

EIGHT

Thomas Sambo

Thomas Sambo is a born again believer who lives in Taraka State, Nigeria, in west Africa.

In 2003, at the age of 23, he experienced heaven and hell. At that time, he was studying veterinary medicine at a university in Borno State, Nigeria.

Before going to hell, Thomas visited heaven with Jesus Christ, receiving glorious revelations from the Lord and Savior. After his visit to heaven, he went to hell.

Two angels accompanied him to hell. Thomas writes: "I cannot vividly describe hell and the sufferings of its occupants. The words to use to describe the nature of hell and the degree of the torments and sufferings of its victims are not available to man on earth."

He explains that just as it is impossible to describe the beauty of heaven, it is impossible to describe the horrors of hell.

Hell scared him. He lost his strength and fell down. He heard the agonizing cries of the damned. They cried out, "Have mercy on us, Lord. Have mercy on us, Lord . . ."

People were crying and gnashing their teeth. It seemed like people were swimming inside flames of hell. He saw the burning flames of fire with people in them – men, women, children; educated, uneducated, rich, poor. "Their breathing was that of gasping for air as one in his dying moment." There is no air in hell, so they are breathing in the flame of fire.

The remembrance of their opportunities to accept Jesus Christ as Savior adds to their torment and sorrow.

Thomas saw fallen angels with whips, beating and tormenting souls. The angels had wickedness on their faces. There were worms in hell, boring their way through the peoples' bodies. The flames did not affect the worms.

Jesus wept: "I formed these people for My glory, but they are now languishing in the eternal torments of hell."

Thomas asked Jesus: "You love man with an everlasting love; but why did you create hell like this?"

Jesus answered: "Hell fire was created only for the devil and his angels. But man put himself in the condition of the devil, so he must suffer the same condemnation."

Jesus said: "I passed through bitter experiences on earth because of the love I have for man. But with all the love I showed man, he rejected Me; that is why he finds himself in hell like this."

At that, Thomas was taken back to heaven and commissioned to tell the world about: Jesus' everlasting love; the need to repent and turn to Jesus Christ; and the importance of truth, righteousness, and holiness.

Thomas was taken to heaven more than once. There, he saw the beauty and glory of heaven, was commissioned by Jesus, and received glorious revelation.

Jesus warned Thomas about sin in the church and the importance of preaching the word and being a pilgrim, a stranger in the world (Ezekiel 8:4-18).

Thomas went to a mansion where he saw many crowns of various sizes. Jesus: "These crowns are for the faithful and overcomers who overcome self, the world and the devil. Blessed are the overcomers for they shall sit at My Father's right hand" (Revelation 2:10b).

Jesus brought him to Thomas' best friend's home in heaven, where they were reunited. Jesus encouraged Thomas to "serve Me in righteousness and holiness . . . amidst this corrupt and perverse generation . . ."

In his second trip, Jesus showed him some things that the Lord restricted Thomas from speaking about. At other times, angels silenced Thomas when he asked questions about certain things.

Then Jesus took him back to hell. They arrived at the gate. Thomas saw multitudes walking on the broad way to hell. He heard the groaning and crying of the damned. He heard their confession of sins that they refused to confess on earth.

Thomas learned that there many pastors and ministers are in hell. Atheists and various categories of humans are also facing eternity in hell.

Jesus: "I created them and loved them with an everlasting love, but they hated Me . . . If any desires to come to heaven, I will give him every grace he needs to come to heaven. But if any desires to go to hell, Satan will immediately give him all the support he needs to be there."

Thomas saw a man from his church who was very zealous for the Lord. Thomas was very surprised this man was in hell. The man said: "I committed fornication and covered it and death came and carried me away" (Proverbs 28:13).

Jesus: "Man cannot understand the nature of the torments of hell. However, go and tell him. Tell him if all the sufferings of the earth were gathered together to be borne by one man, it would still not compare to what that man will suffer for 24 hours in hell."

Jesus warned about believers being careless, worldly, and ungrateful for blessings. He said the church must awake from sleep and save dying men from going to hell.

In his third visit to hell, Thomas met specific people, such as: a woman who dressed provocatively in her church; a woman who was a believer but backslid and died in 2001; a man who had been in hell for thousands of years and knew he was doomed for eternity; a woman who recently ended up in hell and thought she was dreaming but then realized it was real; a man who was an elder in a church but not a born again believer, did not have a genuine salvation from sin through Jesus; a man who was an atheist on earth; a man who was a fornicator and caused women to get abortions; a relative who was religious on earth and who worked for the Lord but did not have a definite experience of salvation from sin through Jesus; and finally, a young child of about 10 years old pleading for mercy.

Jesus allowed Thomas to see how Satan plans certain things to try to deceive people and even believers into leaving the way of holiness and following worldly things. The devil also encourages people to be careless, lazy, and lukewarm toward prayer and the word. The enemy influences people to fornicate and backslide; and he utilizes many other strategies to keep people from following closely behind Jesus.

The standard for heaven is holiness, righteousness, and truth.

NINE

Choo Thomas

Choo Thomas (d. 2013) was a Korean-American who lived in Tacoma, Washington, USA. During her life-time, Jesus showed her heaven and hell.

Thoma was married with two children and two grandchildren. Growing up in Korea, her family was not Christian, and she did not know about Jesus Christ. Choo became a follower of Jesus Christ in 1992 after attending a church several times.

In 1996 and after, Jesus visited Thomas numerous times and revealed heaven and hell to her. Her experiences are recorded in the book *Heaven is So Real*.

Jesus regularly visited Choo, appearing with His person, presence, and anointing.

During these visits, Choo's spirit person would be transported from where she was in the natural (such as her home) to a different place, such as the beach, heaven, or hell.

In an early experience, Jesus took Choo to a beach, then through a large tunnel, and then high up in the air to what he told her is the kingdom. It was a beautiful place where Jesus was on the throne, wearing a radiant gown and a golden crown. Jesus: "The only ones who will go there are the obedient and pure-hearted children. Tell My children to preach the gospel. I am coming soon for those who are waiting and ready for Me."

Jesus explained the work he had called her to.

In further visits, Jesus continued to take Thomas to heaven, showing her that glorious place which is so wonderful and beautiful it cannot be put into human words. They would visit buildings and homes, enjoy the heavenly beauty of rivers, trees, and God-made structures, watch angels at work, and more.

Jesus also showed her hell.

Jesus led Thomas to an area outside the gates of the kingdom. They began to ascend a mountain, going higher and higher, with the road becoming rougher and rougher. They stayed on this narrow road for a long time. Eventually it led to a dark tunnel which they went through. Emerging from the tunnel, they were high up on a hillside. To Thomas, it seemed strange that heaven would have such a dark tunnel and rough road.

They reached the summit, and Thomas looked over the crest of the mountain. She could see fumes and dark smoke rising from a deep pit. It was like the crater of a volcano. Inside it, she could see flames scorching a multitude of people. They were screaming and crying in agony that only the severely burned know.

The people were naked, without hair, and standing close to each other, moving like worms. They could not escape. The walls of the pit were too deep for them to climb. Also, hot coals of fire were all around the edges of the pit.

Choo knew she was standing at the brink of hell. Jesus did not have to tell her. It was even more horrible than the description the Bible gives (example: Revelation 20:13-15).

The flames would leap unexpectedly from all directions. People would move away from flames, and as soon as they thought they were safe, another fire would burst forth. There was no rest for these unfortunate victims. They were doomed to spend all eternity being scorched and burned as they tried to escape.

Choo asked who the people are. Jesus: "My daughter, these people did not know Me."

Jesus made this statement with a voice that heaved with grief. Choo could tell that Jesus was not pleased by the sight in front of them. It bothered Him deeply. Choo knew that Jesus had no control over the destinies of people who choose to reject Him.

Thomas realized her mission was to tell people about the reality of heaven and hell, though they likely would not believe her.

Choo wondered about her own parents, who had never given their hearts to Jesus.

Jesus: "I'm sorry, my daughter. There is nothing I can do for those who do not know Me." Jesus' voice was very sad when saying this.

The reality that her parents were in hell stung Choo. She sobbed the whole time Jesus showed her the scenes of hell.

Jesus touched her head and took her by the hand. He led her down a dark tunnel, then to another rough road that ran very far, to the edge of the pit. They got to the top of the mountain. Choo looked out over a brown and lifeless valley. The whole area was filled with dead grass.

People were wearing sand-colored robes and roaming aimlessly near the pit's mouth. Their heads were low, and they looked dejected and hopeless.

Jesus: "They are disobedient 'Christians.'" He explained they would have to live there forever; that many so-called Christians on earth do not live by His word; they think going to church once a week is enough.

Jesus talked with Choo about her calling and other important aspects of walking Him. Jesus: "Tell everyone that I am ready for whoever is ready and waiting for me."

TEN

Bill Wiese

In 1998, Jesus allowed believer Bill Wiese to experience hell and commissioned him to tell others about it. Jesus also told him to tell others about Jesus' imminent return. In his book *23 Minutes in Hell*, Wiese gives a very descriptive account of the horrors of hell and his terrifying experience there.

Wiese is a dedicated follower of Jesus Christ and has served in ministry for many years. In his professional life, he is a home Realtor. He and his wife Annette live in Southern California, USA. At the time of the experience, Bill was a young man.

There are numerous online videos of Wiese giving his testimony about his experience in hell.

In the middle of the night, at 3 AM to be exact, God took Wiese to hell. At first, Wiese had no idea what was going on. He quickly realized he was lost in hell. He had no memory of his relationship with God. God blocked his memory of being a follower of Jesus, a Christian.

Wiese was sucked out of his body and began falling into a large tunnel. As he fell, it was getting hotter and hotter and hotter. He entered into an open cavern area.

He landed on a stone floor of hell. He looked up and saw iron bars and rough-hewn stone walls. He was in a prison cell. It was like a dungeon.

Bill was paralyzed with fear, panic, terror, and more. Yet his very sharp and keen senses and his understanding allowed him to perceive things on a deep level. He had knowledge that there were different levels of torment and punishment (Matthew 23:14, Matthew 10:15, Hebrews 10:28).

He also knew that some of the things he was experiencing were a thousand times worse than what was possible on earth, such as the strength of the demons and the odors.

He knew that he was deep in the earth.

He was fully awake and could not believe what was happening (Isaiah 24:22, Proverbs 7:27, Job 17:16).

In the cell, he was face down. The heat was unbearable. He had no strength in his body (Isaiah 14:9,10. Psalm 88:4).

Wiese sat up and saw two enormous beasts. They were reptile-like, with bumps and scales, huge jaws, and claws about a foot long. They were about 12 or 13 feet tall. The two beasts were pacing in the cell, with vicious anger, exuding hatred for God. They were two demons.

Then one of them grabbed Bill. The beast threw him into the walls. The other demon dug his claws into Wiese's chest. The Lord allowed him to feel a small amount of pain, enough that it was horrible.

Bill clearly had a body. There was no blood coming from his wounds. He realized later that there is nothing living in hell, so there is no blood (Luke 16, Leviticus 17:11, Zechariah 9:11).

Then it became pitch black dark. God's presence previously lit where Bill was. It was a darkness you could feel. The darkness "had a distinctive evil presence, a feeling of death, a penetrating evil" (Wiese, 9)

Wiese recalls that in hell, there is only hatred and wickedness. The fear penetrates through every cell of your body (Lamentations 3:6, Jude 13).

He was suddenly taken out of the holding cell and appeared next to an enormous pit with raging flames, raining fire, and an unbearable heat. Wiese could see people in the flames, desperately trying to claw their way out. Their screams were "deafening and relentless." He also saw people confined to a pit surrounded by demons.

The walls around him were covered with thousands of hideous creatures with a hatred for mankind. To the right of the large inferno, Wiese could see thousands of small pits, as far as he could see (Psalm 11:6, Psalm 140:10, Matthew 13:49, Revelation 9:2).

He saw people in the flames, with flesh falling off their bones. It was horrible to see. They were screaming and burning. The screams were so loud, he wanted to get away. It was deafening (Psalm 49:14, Isaiah 57:15, Isaiah 32:18).

Wiese writes: "This place was so terrifying, so intense, and so hostile that it would be impossible for me to exaggerate the horror" (9).

In his book, Bill explains in detail the depth of his suffering and terror, such as: the two massive beasts which crushed his body; the raging inferno of lava-like fire; the screams of the untold multitudes; the foul, nauseating, toxic stench; his insatiable thirst and dryness; the total lack of any life whatsoever – no water, nothing living, wounds on his body with no blood; the oxygen-depleted atmosphere; the lack of any compassion or care; no contact with people; and more.

Wiese explains in his teachings and messages that in hell, a person cannot talk to anyone. Every person is isolated. It is a useless wasting away. There is no purpose and no destiny (Ecclesiastes 9:10, Ecclesiastes 6:4, Psalm 88:12).

The smells are incredibly foul, putrid, and disgusting. The stench includes the smell of sulfur, which is a stinking, rotten eggs funk. Wiese points out that on earth, at volcanoes, the toxicity of the sulfur is dangerous and toxic and can kill you. Sulfur is another name for brimstone.

While in hell, Wiese wondered how he could survive.

He felt turmoil and confusion. He wanted to sleep. Though he spent only 23 minutes in hell, it felt like 23 hours. He was totally exhausted (Revelation 14:11, Isaiah 57:20).

All around the massive cavern or chasm, the walls had demonic creatures on them. The demons were all shapes and sizes. They were twisted and deformed, horrible looking, and grotesquely ugly. In terms of their size, most of them were two to 12 feet tall. Some were like spiders about three or four feet across (Revelation 9).

Snakes and maggots were everywhere. There were millions of snakes, maggots, and worms (Isaiah 14:11, Job 24:20).

Wiese was very hungry, yet in hell, people will never, ever get to eat or drink again.

The fear level was beyond anything he could imagine or describe. To get a general estimate of the fear, take any fear on earth and multiply it times 1,000.

How could there be a place like hell?

Wiese tries to answer the question, how could there be a place like hell? Why is it there?

God created the heavens and the earth. Jesus said that God "prepared" hell (Matthew 25:41); the original translation of prepared is "made it ready." That is, God did not "make" hell; He removed his attributes from it. Hell has none of God's attributes. For example, in hell, there is no light, life, love, mercy, strength, water, or peace. See the following scriptures:

Matthew 25:41, John 14:2

James 1:17- Every good and perfect gift comes from the Father

Light – 1 John 1:5

Life – John 1:4

Love – 1 John 4:16

Mercy – Psalm 36:5

Strength – Psalm 18:32

Water – Deuteronomy 11:11

Peace – Isaiah 9:6

Suddenly, Bill began to rise up, and a burst of light invaded the tunnel he was in. The light was a brilliant, pure, white light such as he had never seen. Jesus said, "I AM," and Wiese fell at His feet.

Jesus then talked with Wiese, explaining the experience and the calling Jesus had for him.

Wiese explains that Jesus allowed Wiese to feel and experience "just a small amount of the sorrow He feels for His creation that is going to hell" (36).

Jesus showed Wiese a steady stream of people falling through a tunnel, into the terror Wiese had just escaped. Jesus told him twice, "Tell them I am coming very, very soon!" (38)

ELEVEN

Victoria Nehale

Victoria Nehale lives in Namibia, in southwest Africa. Namibia is a country of 2 million people, bordered by Zambia, Angola, Botswana, South Africa, and the Atlantic Ocean.

Victoria found Jesus Christ as her Lord and Savior on February 6, 2005.

The Lord Jesus Christ has visited her 33 times, and she has visited hell twice.

On July 23, 2005, Victoria went to the town Ondangwa to visit her parents.

While she was lying down at about 6 pm, a heavy anointing came upon her, and she saw Jesus. A brilliant light radiated from Him. He had beautiful tanned skin. His face was full of glory, so much so that she could not look into His eyes. Waves of love emanated from Him.

He extended His hand to her and said, "Victoria, I

want you to come with me; I will show you frightening things and I am taking you to a place where you have never been . . ."

It felt like they were walking on air and ascending. They arrived at a place that was very dry, worse than any desert, with no sign of life whatsoever. It was very depressing.

Jesus said, "We will enter through the gate and the things you will see will frighten and upset you – but you must rest assured that wherever I take you, you will be protected . . ."

Terrified, she started to weep and protest, pleading that He would take her back. Jesus said, "Peace be with you; I am with you. We must go inside, for time is fast running out."

They entered the gate.

Victoria: "I cannot describe to you the horror of that place. I am convinced that there is no other place in the entire universe as bad as that place. The place was extremely large and I had the sense that it was expanding all the time.

"It was a place of utmost darkness and the heat of it could not be measured: it was hotter than the hottest of fires . . . [There were] flies of all sizes – green, black, and grey flies . . . There were also short, thick, black worms everywhere, climbing on everything. The worms started to climb on us and the flies were also all over us.

"The place was filled with the most disgusting stench; there are no words to describe the intensity of the stench of that place. The smell was almost like rotten meat but was a hundred times worse than the most decaying meat . . . The place was filled with the noise of wailing and gnashing of teeth, as well as of demonic, evil laughter.

"The worst thing about this place is that it was filled with people. There were so many people that they could not be numbered. The people were in the form of skeletons. I can say with confidence that these skeletons were humans because I recognized some of my very close relatives and people from my village. Their bones were dark gray and extremely dry. They had long sharp teeth like wild animals. Their mouths were large and wide and their tongues were long and bright red. Their hands and feet had long, thin toes and fingers with long, sharp nails. Some of them had tails and horns.

"There were demons mingling with the people: the demons looked like alligators, and they were walking on four legs. They were comfortable in that environment and were constantly teasing and tormenting the humans. The noise the demons were making was more like a celebration, as they seemed happy and carefree; they were also dancing and jumping all the time.

"The humans, on the other hand, looked miserable and depressed; they were in a state of helplessness and hopelessness. The noise from humans was caused by pain; they were weeping, screaming and gnashing their teeth. They were in a desperate situation of unimaginable pain and agony.

"The people in this place were innumerable, but I could clearly see that the vast majority of them were women. They were divided into many different groups, though it was still not possible to estimate the number of people in any single group because the groups were extremely large.

"Jesus led me to one of the groups on the east side of the place. He said, 'This is a group of people who refused to forgive others. I told them many times in many different ways to forgive others but they rejected me; I have forgiven them all their sins, but they refused to forgive others. Their time ran out, and they found themselves here. They will be here for all eternity; they are eating the fruits of their labor forever and ever. However, it is painful for me to see them in this horrible place and in this situation – because I love them.'"

Victoria saw people she knew from earth, including two close female relatives, a Pastor, her ex-boyfriend, and neighbors. Many of those people cursed her and shouted obscenities at her.

Nehale was petrified and extremely sad. Her body was shaking, and she could not stand. She was crying uncontrollably. Jesus gave her a hug and said, "Peace be with you, Victoria." Her strength returned, and she felt secure.

Jesus told Victoria, "Now you must choose in which of the groups you want to be; the choice is in your own hands." Jesus told her to tell the people on earth everything she had seen but not add or omit anything.

". . . I opened my eyes and was back in my physical body, lying in Oshakati Hospital. There was a drip in my left arm, and I saw my mother and other neighbors from our village in one corner of the room, where they were looking at me in amazement."

The doctor did not know what had happened to Victoria. Her temperature, pulse, and blood pressure were dangerously low, but he did not know the cause. He actually could not admit her, because she was not ill.

Nehale was frightened by what she saw and could not stop crying. The scenes were flashing before her all the time. She could not sleep. Her entire body was in pain. She felt awful. It was almost as if her limbs had been taken apart and reassembled. She had diarrhea and a pounding headache for a week. The awful stench continued to be as real as when she was there.

Victoria decided not to tell anyone about it. But three days later, a mentor called her, and Nehale told the woman about the experience.

On August 19, Victoria felt the anointing as she woke up. She felt waves of electricity going through her body. In the evening, a man in a brilliant light entered her room. He said, "I am Jesus Christ, your Savior. If you have any doubts, look at my hands. That place where we went is hell." She saw scars where the nail pierced Him.

Victoria could not understand why Jesus would tell her which group to choose, when she was a born again Christian. The Lord revealed to her that she had unforgiveness in her heart and needed to rectify a situation in which she had utilized a fraudulent diploma to get a job. She repented of these sins and confessed the fraud to the appropriate officials.

Second Visit to Hell

On October 18, 2005, Victoria again visited hell with Jesus. She saw numerous people she knew.

Jesus explained that all sin is sin; that there is no such thing as big sin and small sin.

They saw a middle-aged woman who on earth was a God-fearing and God-loving person and who had served the Lord in many ways, leading many people to Him and helping the poor.

However, she believed the lie of the devil that there are big sins and little sins. Her sins were theft, causing someone else to steal, and grieving the Holy Spirit. The woman in hell would get a friend who worked at a hospital to give the former (the woman in hell) medicine without paying for it.

The Lord went to her many times and told her to stop what she was doing. But she reasoned that her sin was small, and she attributed the warning from Jesus to her own feelings of guilt.

Jesus also visited Victoria and explained to her the importance of being at places at specified times in order to receive the blessings that angels are distributing for that specified time. If someone is late or not there, they will miss the blessings for that day. Jesus warned her about being late for work and especially late to church services; that if she is late without a valid reason, she has forever missed out on her blessings for those days.

TWELVE

Bernarda Fernandez

One morning, Bernada Fernandez was not feeling well and soon felt like she might die. Her husband was at work. She called some friends. She cried out to the Lord.

Suddenly her room was filled with a light like fire. She saw angels descending into and walking in her room. Another being appeared, more marvelous than the angels. He was dressed in white, with "FAITHFUL AND TRUE" written on His chest. Jesus the Christ was in front of her.

Jesus spoke to her and showed her the marks in His hands from His death. He was to take her on a journey.

He stretched out His hands, and she saw a body come out of her physical body. It was her spirit person.

They descended through a tunnel below the earth. Soon Bernada perceived an unbearable smell. The place was dark. She heard people suffering, weeping, and screaming. She wept and wept. Jesus told her: "Hold on to what you have seen, and do not forget it."

Jesus would not let Bernada see family in hell, but he allowed her to see a young man she knew, named Alexander. Before he died, God had directed Bernada to warn him to repent of his sin.

Jesus showed her thousands of people suffering in hell. He said: "Know that the way to heaven is very narrow, and it will be narrower again. There will be difficulties on earth, so that you will be as pure as gold, but fear not for I am ahead of you like a mighty warrior."

As they got near the lake of fire, Jesus explained He did not prepare it for men, "but all those who do not believe in me as their Savior and those who do not live according to My word will go there."

Jesus was weeping. He said, "There are too many of those who are lost than those who go to heaven."

THIRTEEN

Angelica Zambrano

Angelica Zambrano lives in Ecuador, South America and is a follower of Jesus Christ. She and her mother Maxima attend "Casa de Oracion" Church in their hometown of El Empalme, which is in the province of Guayas in western Ecuador.

Both Angelica and her mother are spirit-filled believers with a passion for Jesus Christ. Before she experienced hell, Angelica had mighty experiences with angels and the Holy Spirit.

While in prayer, suddenly, everything started to move. The earth shook and split open. She began to descend into a very dark hole, which she realized was a tunnel going down into the earth.

Jesus told her not to fear. In a split second, they descended into a terrible darkness, where she heard millions of voices. It was so hot, she felt like her skin was burning. It was the tunnel to hell. There was a horrible, repulsive, and nauseating smell.

Jesus said she needed to go there "so you can tell the

truth to humanity; humanity perishes, it's lost and few are entering My Kingdom." Jesus wept when he said those words, which strengthened Angelica.

Arriving at the end of the tunnel, she looked down and saw an abyss covered in flames. They started to ascend into the abyss. She saw demons of all types, large and small, running fast and carrying things in their hands. Jesus explained that they are hurrying because they know their time is short to deceive humanity. Jesus wept much when explaining how demons deceive people so that people will end up in hell for eternity.

As they walked, they came upon a cell with a young man being tormented among the flames. He had the number "666" on his forehead. Worms were eating him. He begged Jesus to take him out of that place.

Jesus cited John 12:48, saying: "Daughter, he is in this place because anyone who rejects My word already has a judge: the word that I have spoken will judge him in that last day."

Jesus explained that man ends up in hell because of sin and lack of repentance, and "there are more that perish than those who reach My glory." He said:

"I gave My life for humanity, so that it would not perish, so that it would not end up in this place. I gave My life out of love and mercy, so that humanity would proceed to repentance and could enter the Kingdom of Heaven."

They saw another cell, holding a woman who had worms eating her face and demons plunging a spear into her body. She screamed to be let out.

Angelica realized that people in hell are also tormented with the memories of what they did on earth. Demons would mock them, "Worship and praise because this is your kingdom!" Those in hell who knew God and the word were tormented twofold.

They met a relative of Angelica's in hell (her great-grandmother). Jesus explained that this woman is in hell because she did not forgive: "He who does not forgive, neither will I forgive him . . . many people are in this place, because they failed to forgive. Tell them to rid themselves of grudges, of resentment, of that hatred in their hearts, for it is time to forgive!"

Many people extended their arms out, begging Jesus to help them and take them out. They would blaspheme Jesus, who said: "It hurts Me to hear them, it hurts Me to see what they do, because I can no longer do anything for them."

As they moved on, Angelica saw an area where many former singers and artists were kept. Jesus explained that people in hell have to continue doing what they did on earth. If they sang, they have to keep singing and singing.

The demons sent down fire and brimstone like rain and taunted those in hell, telling them: "Praise and worship because this is your kingdom forever and ever!" Jesus said: "This is the wages of anyone who has not repented."

Jesus explained that he chose Angelica to be a watchman, to tell the truth, to tell people all that He has shown her. He also explained that if she does not speak out and something happens to a person, "his blood will be poured over you . . ." (Ezekiel 3:18).

She asked Jesus how people who knew Him could end up in hell. Jesus replied, "That person who has left My ways and that person who is living a double life."

He told her, "Many will not believe you, but I am your faithful witness. I will never leave you. Even if they don't believe you, Daughter, go and tell them the truth, for I am with you."

They saw a tunnel where a multitude of people were falling into the abyss. Jesus wept as they saw countless people falling by the second, "like handfuls of sand being thrown down."

He explained how demons have meetings, "daily secret meetings," planning how they will go and destroy people of God.

FOURTEEN

Every Scripture about Hell and the Worlds Under the Earth

In the Bible, there are more than 100 verses about the five worlds under the earth: hell, the pit, tartarus, the lake of fire, and paradise. The vast majority of the scriptures are about hell, also called Hades and Sheol. A full summary of these five worlds are on pages 128-136.

Hell – where lost, unsaved souls go after death
The Pit – the home of demons
Tartarus – where fallen angels are kept in chains
Lake of fire – where hell will be for eternity
Paradise – where pre-resurrection saints went

Then Jacob . . . mourned for his son many days. And all his sons and all his daughters arose to comfort him; but he refused to be comforted, and he said, 'For I shall go down into the grave [Sheol, hell] to my son in mourning.'
Genesis 37:34-35

But if the Lord creates a new thing, and the earth opens its mouth and swallows them up with all that belongs to them, and they go down alive into the pit, then you will understand that these men have rejected the Lord.

Numbers 16:30

So they and all those with them went down alive into the pit; the earth closed over them, and they perished from among the assembly.

Numbers 16:33

For a fire is kindled in My anger, and shall burn to the lowest hell; It shall consume the earth with her increase, and set on fire the foundations of the mountains.

Deuteronomy 32:22

He made a pit and dug it out, and has fallen into the ditch which he made.

Psalm 7:15

The nations have sunk down in the pit which they made; In the net which they hid, their own foot is caught.

Psalm 9:15

The wicked shall be turned into hell, and all the nations that forget God.

Psalm 9:17

For You will not leave my soul in Sheol, Nor will You allow Your Holy One to see corruption.

Psalm 16:10

The sorrows of Sheol surrounded me; The snares of death confronted me.
Psalm 18:5

To You I will cry, O Lord my Rock: Do not be silent to me, Lest, if You are silent to me, I become like those who go down to the pit.
Psalm 28:1

O Lord, You brought my soul up from the grave; You have kept me alive, that I should not go down to the pit.
Psalm 30:3

"What profit is there in my blood, When I go down to the pit? Will the dust praise You? Will it declare Your truth?
Psalm 30:9

For without cause they have hidden their net for me in a pit, which they have dug without cause for my life.
Psalm 35:7

He also brought me up out of a horrible pit, out of the miry clay, And set my feet upon a rock, And established my steps.
Psalm 40:2

That he should continue to live eternally, and not see the Pit
Psalm 49:9

Let death seize them; Let them go down alive into hell, for wickedness is in their dwellings and among them.
Psalm 55:15

But You, O God, shall bring them down to the pit of destruction; Bloodthirsty and deceitful men shall not live out half their days; But I will trust in You.
    Psalm 55:23

They have prepared a net for my steps; My soul is bowed down; They have dug a pit before me; Into the midst of it they themselves have fallen.
    Psalm 57:6

Let not the floodwater overflow me, nor let the deep swallow me up; And let not the pit shut its mouth on me.
    Psalm 69:15

For great is Your mercy toward me, And You have delivered my soul from the depths of Sheol.
    Psalm 86:13

I am counted with those who go down to the pit; I am like a man who has no strength,
    Psalm 88:4

You have laid me in the lowest pit, In darkness, in the depths.
    Psalm 88:6

That You may give him rest from the days of adversity, Until the pit is dug for the wicked.
    Psalm 94:13

The pains of death surrounded me, And the pangs of Sheol laid hold of me; I found trouble and sorrow.
    Psalm 116:3

If I ascend into heaven, you are there; If I make my bed in hell, behold, you are there.
Psalm 139:8

Answer me speedily, O Lord; My spirit fails! Do not hide Your face from me, Lest I be like those who go down into the pit.
Psalm 143:7

Surely by now he is hidden in some pit, or in some other place. And it will be, when some of them are overthrown at the first, that whoever hears it will say, 'There is a slaughter among the people who follow Absalom.'
2 Samuel 17:9

And they took Absalom and cast him into a large pit in the woods, and laid a very large heap of stones over him. Then all Israel fled, everyone to his tent.
2 Samuel 18:17

The sorrows of Sheol surrounded me; the snares of death confronted me.
2 Samuel 22:6

Yet You will plunge me into the pit, and my own clothes will abhor me.
Job 9:31

They are higher than heaven— what can you do? Deeper than Sheol— what can you know?
Job 11:8

Will they go down to the gates of Sheol? Shall we have rest together in the dust?"

Job 17:16

Sheol is naked before Him, And Destruction has no covering.
Job 26:6

He keeps back his soul from the Pit, And his life from perishing by the sword.
Job 33:18

Yes, his soul draws near the Pit, And his life to the executioners.
Job 33:22

Then He is gracious to him, and says, 'Deliver him from going down to the Pit; I have found a ransom';
Job 33:24

He will redeem his soul from going down to the Pit, And his life shall see the light.
Job 33:28

To bring back his soul from the Pit, that he may be enlightened with the light of life.
Job 33:30

Let us swallow them alive like Sheol, and whole, like those who go down to the Pit;
Proverbs 1:12

Her feet go down to death, her steps lay hold of hell.
Proverbs 5:5

Her house is the way to hell, descending to the chambers of death.
Proverbs 7:27

But he does not know that the dead are there, that her guests are in the depths of hell.
Proverbs 9:18

Hell and Destruction are before the Lord; So how much more the hearts of the sons of men.
Proverbs 15:11

The way of life winds upward for the wise, that he may turn away from hell below.
Proverbs 15:24

The mouth of an immoral woman is a deep pit. He who is abhorred by the Lord will fall there.
Proverbs 22:14

You shall beat him with a rod, and deliver his soul from hell.
Proverbs 23:14

For a harlot is a deep pit, and a seductress is a narrow well.
Proverbs 23:27

Whoever digs a pit will fall into it, and he who rolls a stone will have it roll back on him.
Proverbs 26:27

Hell and Destruction are never full; So the eyes of man are never satisfied.
Proverbs 27:20

Whoever causes the upright to go astray in an evil way, He himself will fall into his own pit; But the

blameless will inherit good.
  Proverbs 28:10

He who digs a pit will fall into it, and whoever breaks
through a wall will be bitten by a serpent.
  Ecclesiastes 10:8

Therefore Sheol has enlarged itself, and opened its
mouth beyond measure; their glory and their multitude and their pomp, and he who is jubilant, shall descend into it.
  Isaiah 5:14

Your pomp is brought down to Sheol, And the sound
of your stringed instruments; The maggot is spread
under you, and worms cover you.'
  Isaiah 14:11

Hell from beneath is excited about you, To meet
you at your coming; It stirs up the dead for you, All
the chief ones of the earth; It has raised up from their
thrones All the kings of the nations.
  Isaiah 14:9

Yet you shall be brought down to Sheol, To the lowest depths of the Pit.
  Isaiah 14:15

But you are cast out of your grave like an abominable
branch, Like the garment of those who are slain, Thrust
through with a sword, Who go down to the stones of
the pit, like a corpse trodden underfoot.
  Isaiah 14:19

Fear and the pit and the snare Are upon you, O in-

habitant of the earth.
    Isaiah 24:17

And it shall be that he who flees from the noise of the
fear shall fall into the pit, and he who comes up from
the midst of the pit shall be caught in the snare; For the
windows from on high are open, And the foundations
of the earth are shaken.
    Isaiah 24:18

They will be gathered together, as prisoners are gathered in the pit, and will be shut up in the prison; After
many days they will be punished.
    Isaiah 24:22

Because you have said, "We have made a covenant
with death, And with Sheol we are in agreement.
When the overflowing scourge passes through, it will
not come to us, For we have made lies our refuge, And
under falsehood we have hidden ourselves.
    Isaiah 28:15

Your covenant with death will be annulled, and your
agreement with Sheol will not stand; When the overflowing scourge passes through, Then you will be
trampled down by it.
    Isaiah 28:18

I said, "In the prime of my life I shall go to the gates
of Sheol; I am deprived of the remainder of my years."
    Isaiah 38:10

Indeed it was for my own peace that I had great bit-
terness; But You have lovingly delivered my soul from
the pit of corruption, For You have cast all my sins be-

hind Your back.
  Isaiah 38:17

For Sheol cannot thank You, Death cannot praise
You; Those who go down to the pit cannot hope for
Your truth.
  Isaiah 38:18

You went to the king with ointment, and increased
your perfumes; You sent your messengers far off, And
even descended to Sheol.
  Isaiah 57:9

"And they shall go forth and look upon the corps-
es of the men who have transgressed against Me. For
their worm does not die, and their fire is not quenched.
They shall be an abhorrence to all flesh."
  Isaiah 66:24

Though they dig into hell, From there My hand shall
take them; Though they climb up to heaven, From
there I will bring them down;
  Amos 9:2

And he said: "I cried out to the Lord because of my
affliction, And He answered me. "Out of the belly of
Sheol I cried, And You heard my voice."
  Jonah 2:2

[Woe to the Wicked] Indeed, because he transgresses
by wine, He is a proud man, And he does not stay at
home. Because he enlarges his desire as hell, And he is
like death, and cannot be satisfied, He gathers to himself
all nations And heaps up for himself all peoples.
  Habakkuk 2:5

Thus says the Lord God: 'In the day when it went down to hell, I caused mourning. I covered the deep because of it. I restrained its rivers, and the great waters were held back. I caused Lebanon to mourn for it, and all the trees of the field wilted because of it.
Ezekiel 31:15

I made the nations shake at the sound of its fall, when I cast it down to hell together with those who descend into the Pit; and all the trees of Eden, the choice and best of Lebanon, all that drink water, were comforted in the depths of the earth.
Ezekiel 31:16

They also went down to hell with it, with those slain by the sword; and those who were its strong arm dwelt in its shadows among the nations.
Ezekiel 31:17

The strong among the mighty shall speak to him out of the midst of hell with those who help him: 'They have gone down, they lie with the uncircumcised, slain by the sword.'
Ezekiel 32:21

They do not lie with the mighty Who are fallen of the uncircumcised, who have gone down to hell with their weapons of war; They have laid their swords under their heads, but their iniquities will be on their bones, Because of the terror of the mighty in the land of the living.
Ezekiel 32:27

"But I say to you that whoever is angry with his

brother without a cause shall be in danger of the judgment. And whoever says to his brother, 'Raca!' shall be in danger of the council. But whoever says, 'You fool!' shall be in danger of hell fire."
Matthew 5:22

"If your right eye causes you to sin, pluck it out and cast it from you; for it is more profitable for you that one of your members perish, than for your whole body to be cast into hell."
Matthew 5:29

"And if your right hand causes you to sin, cut it off and cast it from you; for it is more profitable for you that one of your members perish, than for your whole body to be cast into hell."
Matthew 5:30

"But the sons of the kingdom will be cast out into outer darkness. There will be weeping and gnashing of teeth."
Matthew 8:12

"And do not fear those who kill the body but cannot kill the soul. But rather fear Him who is able to destroy both soul and body in hell."
Matthew 10:28

"And you, Capernaum, who are exalted to heaven, will be brought down to Hades; for if the mighty works which were done in you had been done in Sodom, it would have remained until this day."
Matthew 11:23

"For as Jonah was three days and three nights in the

belly of the great fish, so will the Son of Man be three days and three nights in the heart of the earth."
Matthew 12:40

"The Son of Man will send out His angels, and they will gather out of His kingdom all things that offend, and those who practice lawlessness, and will cast them into the furnace of fire. There will be wailing and gnashing of teeth."
Matthew 13:41

"And I also say to you that you are Peter, and on this rock I will build My church, and the gates of Hades shall not prevail against it."
Matthew 16:18

"And if your eye causes you to sin, pluck it out and cast it from you. It is better for you to enter into life with one eye, rather than having two eyes, to be cast into hell fire."
Matthew 18:9

"Woe to you, scribes and Pharisees, hypocrites! For you travel land and sea to win one proselyte, and when he is won, you make him twice as much a son of hell as yourselves."
Matthew 23:15

"Serpents, brood of vipers! How can you escape the condemnation of hell?"
Matthew 23:33

"But if that evil servant says in his heart, 'My master is delaying his coming,' and begins to beat his fellow servants, and to eat and drink with the drunkards, the

master of that servant will come on a day when he is not looking for him and at an hour that he is not aware of, and will cut him in two and appoint him his portion with the hypocrites. There shall be weeping and gnashing of teeth."
Matthew 24:48-50

"And cast the unprofitable servant into the outer darkness. There will be weeping and gnashing of teeth."
Matthew 25:30

"Then He will also say to those on the left hand, depart from Me, you cursed, into the everlasting fire prepared for the devil and his angels . . ."
Matthew 25:41

"If your hand causes you to sin, cut it off. It is better for your to enter into life maimed, rather than having two hands, to be cast into hell, to go to hell, into the fire shall never be quenched – 'where their worm does not die, and the fire is not quenched.'"
Mark 9:44

And you, Capernaum, who are exalted to heaven, will be brought down to Hades.
Luke 10:15

But I will show you whom you should fear: Fear Him who, after He has killed, has power to cast into hell; yes, I say to you, fear Him!
Luke 12:5

And being in torments in Hades, he lifted up his eyes and saw Abraham afar off, and Lazarus in his bosom.

Then he cried and said, 'Father Abraham, have mercy on me, and send Lazarus that he may dip the tip of his finger in water and cool my tongue; for I am tormented in this flame.'
Luke 16:23-24

For You will not leave my soul in Hades, Nor will You allow Your Holy One to see corruption.
Acts 2:27

He, foreseeing this, spoke concerning the resurrection of the Christ, that His soul was not left in Hades, nor did His flesh see corruption.
Acts 2:31

Now this, "He ascended" – what does it mean but that He also first descended into the lower parts of the earth?
Ephesians 4:9

O Death, where is your sting? O Hades, where is your victory?
1 Corinthians 15:55

And the tongue is a fire, a world of iniquity. The tongue is so set among our members that it defiles the whole body, and sets on fire the course of nature; and it is set on fire by hell.
James 3:6

For if God did not spare the angels who sinned, but cast them down to hell and delivered them into chains of darkness, to be reserved for judgment.
2 Peter 2:4

If your hand causes you to sin, cut it off. It is better for you to enter into life maimed, rather than having two hands, to go to hell, into the fire that shall never be quenched
Mark 9:43

And if your foot causes you to sin, cut it off. It is better for you to enter life lame, rather than having two feet, to be cast into hell, into the fire that shall never be quenched —
Mark 9:45

And if your eye causes you to sin, pluck it out. It is better for you to enter the kingdom of God with one eye, rather than having two eyes, to be cast into hell fire —
Mark 9:47

I am He who lives, and was dead, and behold, I am alive forevermore. Amen. And I have the keys of Hades and of Death.
Revelation 1:18

He who has an ear, let him hear what the Spirit says to the churches. He who overcomes shall not be hurt by the second death.
Revelation 2:11

So I looked, and behold, a pale horse. And the name of him who sat on it was Death, and Hades followed with him. And power was given to them over a fourth of the earth, to kill with sword, with hunger, with death, and by the beasts of the earth.
Revelation 6:8

Then the beast was captured, and with him the false prophet who worked signs in his presence, by which he deceived those who received the mark of the beast and those who worshiped his image. These two were cast alive into the lake of fire burning with brimstone.
Revelation 19:20

Blessed and holy is he who has part in the first resurrection. Over such the second death has no power, but they shall be priests of God and of Christ, and shall reign with Him a thousand years.
Revelation 20:6

The devil, who deceived them, was cast into the lake of fire and brimstone where the beast and the false prophet are. And they will be tormented day and night forever and ever.
Revelation 20:10

The sea gave up the dead who were in it, and Death and Hades delivered up the dead who were in them. And they were judged, each one according to his works.
Revelation 20:13

Then Death and Hades were cast into the lake of fire. This is the second death. And anyone not found written in the Book of Life was cast into the lake of fire.
Revelation 20:14

But the cowardly, unbelieving, abominable, murderers, sexually immoral, sorcerers, idolaters, and all liars shall have their part in the lake which burns with fire and brimstone, which is the second death."
Revelation 21:8

FIFTEEN

Number of People Per Day Who Die and Go to Hell

Answer, an estimate (explanation follows): according to statistics, approximately 83,000 people a day die and go to hell.

Christianity believes in the Lordship of Jesus Christ. Christians could accurately be called "followers of Jesus Christ." Many Christians label their faith as a relationship with God and not at all associated with religion. For discussion sake only, though, world population stats will be presented according to "religion" and include Christianity.

According to world religion statistics, Christianity includes approximately 2.35 billion people, or 31.5% of the world's population.

The world population is 7.48 billion people. The population is increasing by 70 million per year and 200,000 per day. Therefore, by the year 2020, the population will be about 7.7 billion.

Every day, approximately 151,000 people die and 360,000 people are born.

In the effort to figure out how many people of the 151,000 daily deaths make it to heaven, we first need to subtract the 29,000 children under the age of five who die daily. Tragically, these children die due to malnutrition (one-third) and preventable diseases, the main ones being: diarrhea, malaria, neonatal infection, pneumonia, preterm delivery, or lack of oxygen at birth. When these children under the age of about five die, they go directly to heaven. Amen! (Matthew 18:10)

Thus, there are 122,000 people past the "age of accountability" who die every day. The age of accountability is when someone is mature enough to choose whom they serve, through their beliefs, words, and actions. The age of accountability is at about age five.

Let's first be clear: Christians believe that true followers of Jesus Christ will go to heaven, while people who are not followers of Jesus will, tragically, end up in hell for eternity.

This statement is harsh, possibly offensive, and sounds self-righteous. But if we go by the Bible and by the revelation of the Holy Spirit, the only way to get to heaven is through Jesus Christ (John 14:6). This truth is central to Christianity and what makes it unique.

There is only one faith that has a Savior who came to world to die for mankind, who died, rose from the dead, and ascended to heaven where He was before he came to earth and where He is now.

If we go by pure stats, 31.5% of the 122,000, or 38,430 people, make it to heaven daily. The remaining 83,570 people are not, according to world religion statistics, followers of Jesus Christ. They therefore go to hell upon death.

Now, in reality, we know that of the 2.35 billion "Christians" and "Catholics" in the world, not all of them are truly saved. We hope they are. We believe that God is merciful and that "all who call upon the name of the Lord shall be saved" (Joel 2:32, Romans 10:13).

But, the reality is quite different, as this book reveals.

No man knows who is saved or is the judge of humanity. God is of course the only Judge. But it is safe to say that the 83,000 figure for people ending up in hell is conservative. That is, of the 31.5% of Christians in the world, if in reality 80% of those 2.35 billion people are truly saved and will make it to heaven, then the real figure of people going to hell jumps to 100,284 per day.

The 2.35 billion Christians includes 1.2 billion Catholics, 900 million Protestants, and 200 million Orthodox Christians.

World Religion Affiliation	
Christian: Catholic/Protestant	2.35 billion
Islam/Muslim	1.6 billion
Secular/nonreligious	1.1 billion
Hindu	1 billion
Chinese tradition	400 million
Buddhism	380 million
Ethnic religions	300 million
African traditional	100 million
	Source: Pew Research Center

SIXTEEN

The Five Worlds Under the Earth

There are five worlds under the earth:

Hell/Sheol – the place where humans who do not know Jesus Christ as Lord and Savior go upon earthly death; also called hell; located in the center of the earth

The Pit – the home of demons

Tartarus – the place where millions upon millions of angels are kept in prison, in chains

Lake of fire – a literal massive lake of fire; no one is there right now; hell will eventually be thrown into it

Paradise – the place where pre-Christ saints went after dying

The apostle Paul writes about *"those under the earth"* in Philippians:

> "Therefore God also has highly exalted Him and given Him the name which is above every name, that at the name of Jesus every knee should bow, of those in heaven, and of those on earth, and

of those under the earth, and that every tongue should confess that Jesus Christ is Lord, to the glory of God the Father."
(Philippians 2:9-11)

The Five Underworlds and their Inhabitants
Sheol, or Hell

Sheol is the place most commonly referred to as hell. In modern Bibles, the Hebrew word for "Sheol" (used 65 times in the original Bible) is usually translated either "hell" (31 times) or "the grave" (also 31 times). The Greek word for hell is "hades," found 11 times in the Bible.

The Five Underworlds and Their Inhabitants		
Hell, or Sheol	Where lost souls are	76 times in Bible
Lake of fire	Where hell ends up	Revelation 21:8
The Pit	Home of demons	Luke 8:26-39
Tartarus	Angels kept in chains	1 Peter 3:18-20
Paradise	Saints were here	Luke 23:43

Millions upon millions of souls are in Sheol right now, suffering in excruciating, continual torment and torture. Sheol is a place of fire, with flames of fire, waves of fire, hot coals, burning, and smoke. Those in hell suffer from the fires of hell continually, with no relief. They are experiencing eternal death, but they cannot actually die.

They have an eternal spirit; a soul which is their mind, emotions, and will; and a body with flesh that continually burns and falls off their skeleton.

There is loud wailing and weeping, horrible odors,

worms crawling in the peoples' bodies, and many other torments. They have no relief, no comfort, no water, nothing good. In hell, people have all their senses, which are a lot stronger in the afterlife, both in hell and in heaven.

Hell is located in the center of the earth. It is shaped like a human body lying on its back, with arms and legs stretched out. There are many different parts of hell, such as the arms, belly, heart, head, legs, and so forth.

In the Bible, hell is referred to as "under" and "beneath" (see Isaiah 14:9, Ezekiel 31:16, Job 11:8, and many others). There are deep depths to hell (see Deuteronomy 32:22). Hell has gates and has deprived people of their years (see Isaiah 38:10). If someone dies without knowing God through the Savior, that person immediately goes to hell (see Job 21:13).

In recent years, Jesus has revealed much about hell through His people. For a detailed description of hell, see the book *Divine Revelation of Hell* by Mary Baxter.

Paradise

Paradise was the place that pre-resurrection saints went when they died. Today it is empty.

Paradise's description is just like its name: it is a place of beauty, rest, peace, joy, and love.

Before Jesus died and was resurrected, there was no way for saints to go to heaven, so they went to Paradise. Remember Jesus told the thief on the cross, *"Today, you will be with Me in paradise"* (Luke 23:43). Before we discuss that, some background information is needed.

When Jesus Christ died, it was . . . well, that event really cannot be put into human words.

God sent His Son to the earth to die for mankind. It's

beyond human comprehension. The God Who created the universe, the earth, and mankind, sent His Son to die and redeem mankind . . . it's truly a mystery that He would do this.

For all eternity, the sacrifice of Jesus will be honored, proclaimed, revered, celebrated, extolled, and much, much more.

God's children, which He made into His own image, sinned and fell. The Holy God cannot look upon sin. There had to be a perfect sacrifice for man's sins. Jesus is that sacrifice.

Right after Jesus died, some truly incredible things happened.

The veil in front of the Holy of Holies was torn in two from top to bottom.

The Holy of Holies in the Temple and the Tabernacle was the place where the holy, sacred Presence of God dwelt. The construction and building of the Tabernacle is described in Exodus 25. The construction and building of the Temple is described in 1 Kings 6.

The veil in front of the Holy of Holies was a very large, thick curtain that took as many as 300 men to move and put in place. Scholars estimate the veil was between about 30-40 feet tall, 30-40 feet wide, and about four to six inches thick.

What does the tearing of the veil mean? After Jesus died, that Presence became available to all people, not just the High Priest or the select few.

We read in New Testament about more amazing things that happened after Jesus died.

Between His death and His ascension into heaven, Jesus went to the underworld. He went to Paradise and released the saints there to go to heaven. We read about their release in Matthew 27. Note that the phrase "fallen asleep" refers to people who were dead:

> "Then, behold, the veil of the temple was torn in
> two from top to bottom; and the earth quaked,
> and the rocks were split, 52 and the graves were
> opened; and many bodies of the saints who had
> fallen asleep were raised; 53 and coming out of the
> graves after His resurrection, they went into the
> holy city and appeared to many.
> (Matthew 27:51-53)

In the Parable of the Rich Man and Lazarus (Luke 16:19-31), we learn about Paradise, though the story does not actually use the word Paradise. In the translation from Greek to English, the dynamics of the Greek word "kolpos" are the reason there are various translations for the actual place the beggar Lazarus went when he died.

The word "kolpos" is intended to convey "a position synonymous with intimacy." It is also used in John 1:18 describing Jesus Christ's intimacy with the Father.

In the Lazarus Parable, various Bible versions translate the word and phrase "kolpos" in such ways as: "with Abraham", "in the arms of Abraham," "Abraham's side," "Abraham's bosom," and so forth, all describing Paradise.

The Pit

The Pit is the home of demons. Right now, millions upon millions of demons, the pre-Adamic inhabitants of the earth, are in the Pit, also called "the deep" and "the abyss."

Many demons are traveling from the Pit to the earth to try to influence and deceive men and women as well as cause problems on the earth. They try to find humans to live in, which will be their "house" (see Matthew 12:43-45). If they do not find one, they have to return to the Pit.

Demons are just one of five divisions in the devil's army, summarized starting on page 99.

In Luke 8:26-39, we read about Jesus casting demons out of a man. The demons actually begged Jesus not to send them to the Pit (see Luke 8:30).

In Revelation 9:1-12, there is a scary description of the end times when demons will be released from the Pit. The demons are commanded twice not to destroy men, because demons would destroy everything if they could. In verse 11, we read that the one in charge of them is Satan:

> And they had as king over them the angel of the bottomless pit, whose name in Hebrew is Abaddon, but in Greek he has the name Apollyon. (Revelation 9:11)

Remember that Satan and Satan's army are continually trying to deceive mankind into not following God through Jesus Christ, into not becoming children of God. Satan hates God and is trying to win the war in the heavens. His main way of doing this is to influence men and women not to follow Jesus Christ, with the ultimate goal of causing humans to end up in hell, where people will be stuck forever in horrible torment and fire, with the devil.

Hell was created for Satan and his angels, not for human beings. Jesus said:

> Then He will also say to those on the left hand, 'Depart from Me, you cursed, into the everlasting

fire prepared for the devil and his angels: . . .'
(Matthew 27:41)

Satan, his angels, and his demons will spend eternity in hell. Tragically, Satan is deceiving many human beings into also going to hell.

God wants every person to make it to heaven. But He cannot make anyone choose Him or follow Him. How can this be?

Remember the key fact: God made man into His own image and likeness. God gave every person a complete free will to decide every aspect of his or her life, including the god he or she serves. Though God the Father and God the Son want every person to be saved and make it heaven, God cannot make anyone become a child of God. It's a mystery, yet it's a reality.

When a human is a child, before the age of accountability, which is usually around five or six years old, they actually are a child of God. If a child under that age dies, they go to heaven, where they grow up into adults.

So, the devil knows he can influence people, and he and his armies continually try to do this.

Tartarus

Tartarus is the abode of fallen angels that slept with women.

In 2 Peter 2:4ff, Peter connects "hell," which in this passage is the Greek word for Tartarus, to the flood. We learned earlier that the flood in Noah's time was because angels had polluted mankind's seed to the point that God in anger destroyed all mankind except Noah and his family.

In Jude 1:6,7, we read that the angels *"left their habi-*

tation" and slept with women, with *"strange flesh,"* like Sodom and Gomorrah did (see Genesis 19).

In 1 Peter 3:18, we read that Jesus, after he died, went to Tartarus, after He went to Paradise. We also read here about the angels' disobedience during the time of Noah. The words "spirits in prison" below is "angels in Tartarus" in the Greek:

> For Christ also suffered once for sins, the just for the unjust, that He might bring us to God, being put to death in the flesh but made alive by the Spirit, 19 by whom also He went and preached to the spirits in prison, 20 who formerly were disobedient, when once the Divine long suffering waited in the days of Noah, while the ark was being prepared, in which a few, that is, eight souls, were saved through water.
> (I Peter 3:18-20)

He preached to the millions of angels who slept with women, who joined forces with Satan and rebelled against God. They polluted the entire human race except for Noah and tried to stop the Messiah from coming. They thought they had succeeded and that they would one day get out of Tartarus. They have been chained there for thousands of years. Jesus proclaimed to them that He made it and prepared them for Judgment Day.

The Lake of Fire

As we read earlier, the Lake of Fire was created for the devil and his angels. There is no one there right now.

Isaiah 66:24 says that the Lake of Fire will last eternally.

One day, all the inhabitants of the five worlds will be thrown into the lake of fire. The other four worlds will be destroyed. The lake of fire will exist forever.

Notes

Cover Pages

1. Baxter, *A Divine Revelation of Hell*, p. 38
2. Ibid., p. 63
3. Peralta, *Hell Testimonies*, e-book
4. Wiese, *23 Minutes in Hell*, p. 28
5. Peralta, *Hell Testimonies*, e-book
6. Ibid., e-book
7. Yeager, Hell is For Real, e-book
8. Hagin, I Saw Hell, p. 5
9. Peralta, *Hell Testimonies*, e-book
10. Ibid., e-book
11. Ibid., e-book
12. Baxter, *A Divine Revelation of Hell*, p. 37
13. Ibid., p. 42
14. Ibid., p. 44-45
15. Ibid., p. 49
16. Ibid., p. 54
17. Ibid., p. 65
18. Ibid., p. 72
19. Ibid., p. 78
20. Ibid., p. 79
21. Ibid., p. 91
22. Ibid., p. 92
23. Ibid., p. 95
24. Ibid., p. 149

Introduction
1. Baxter, *A Divine Revelation of Hell*, p. 94

Chapter One
1. Baxter, *A Divine Revelation of Hell*, p. 78,

Revelations and Deep Truths (starts on page 23): 1. p. 37, 2. p. 38, 3. p. 42, 4. p. 44-45, 5. p. 49, 6. p. 52, 7. p. 54, 8. p. 60, 9. p. 63, 10. p. 72, 11. p. 78, 12. p. 79, 13. p. 91, 15. p. 92, 16. p. 95, 17. p. 99, 18. p. 100, 19. p. 105, 20. p. 149, Summary: 21. p. 15, 22. p. 16, 23. p. 17, 24. p. 19.

Left Leg (starts on page 29): 1. p. 21, 2. p. 22, 3. p. 24, 4. p. 26, 5. p. 27, 6. p. 28, 7. p. 29, 8. p. 30, 9. p. 33, 10. p. 34-35

Right Leg (starts on page 33): 1. p. 38, 2. p. 39, 3. p. 43, 4. p. 44, 5. p. 44-45, 6. p. 45, 7. p. 45-46

More Pits: 1. p. 49, 2. p. 50, 3. p. 52, 4. p. 52, 5. p. 52, 6. p. 53, 7. p. 53, 8. p. 54, 9. p. 54, 10. p. 54-55, 11. p. 56, 12. p. 56, 13. p. 57, 14. p. 58, 15. p. 59-60, 16. p. 60

Tunnel of Fear: 1. p. 63, 2. p. 64, 3. p. 65

Activity in Hell: 1. p. 67-68, 2. p. 68, 3. p. 69, 4. p. 70, 5. p. 71, 6. p. 72, 7. p. 73, 8. p. 73

The Belly of Hell: 1. p. 78, 2. p. 79, 3. p. 80

The Cells in Hell: 1. p. 82, 2. p. 84, 3. p. 85

The Horrors of Hell:"1. p. 90, 2. p. 91, 3. p. 92, 4. p. 94, 5. p. 95, 6. p. 97, 7. p. 99

The Heart of Hell: 1. p. 103, 2. p. 105, 3. p. 110, 4. p. 111, 5. p. 112, 6. p. 7. 112-113

Outer Darkness: 1. p. 115, 2. p. 116, 3. p. 116, 4. p. 117, 5. p. 117-118

Center of Hell: 1. p. 147, 2. p. 148, 3. p. 149, 4. p. 150, 5. p. 151, 6. p. 153, 7. p. 156,

List of Lost Souls: 1. p. 24, 2. p. 26, 3. p. 28, 4. p. 31, 5. p. 41, 6. p. 44-46, 7. p. 50, 8. p. 52-56, 9. p. 56, 10. p. 59, 11. p. 69, 12. p. 83, 13. p. 108, 14. p. 147, 15. p. 150, 16. p. 151, 17. p. 152, 18. p. 154, 19. p. 155, 20. p. 156

Chapter Two
Hagin, *I Went to Hell*

Chapter Three
Yeager, *Hell is For Real*, ebook

Chapter Four
Kelley, "Boy Died of Drug Overdose and Went to Hell (Hell Testimony) Earthquake Kelley with Sid Roth"

Chapter Five
Ron Reagan, "Atheist Died, Went to Hell, Came Back (Parts 1 and 2)," YouTube, and additional videos

Chapter Six
Carmelo Brenes, Peralta, *Hell Testimonies*

Chapter Seven
Mario Martinez, "Heaven vs. Hell: Mario Martinez sees hell, demons, angels and more, YouTube

Chapter Eight
Thomas Sambo, Peralta, *Hell Testimonies*

Chapter Nine

Choo   Thomas,   ChooThomas.org,   Peralta,   *Hell Testimonies*

Chapter Ten
Bill Wiese, *23 Minutes in Hell*

Chapter Eleven
Victoria Nehale, Peralta, *Hell Testimonies*

Chapter Twelve
Bernarda   Fernandez,   "Prepare   for   the   Lord's Return," by Bernarda Fernandez, Audio, www. divinerevelations.info, and additional sources.

Chapter Thirteen
Angelica Zambrano, Peralta, *Hell Testimonies*

Chapter Sixteen
Sources, population and world religion statistics:
Pew Resource Center,
www.worldometers.info/world-population,
www.worldpopulationbalance.org/
www.worldlifeexpectancy.com/live-world-death-to-tals
www.unicef.org/mdg/childmortality.html

Bibliography

Hagin, Kenneth E. *I Went to Hell* (Tulsa: Rhema Bible Church aka Kenneth Hagin Ministries, 1982).

Wiese, Bill. *23 Minutes in Hell* (Lake Mary, FL: Charisma House, 2006).

Peralta, Mike. *Hell Testimonies* (Mike Peralta, 2012).

Baxter, Mary K. *A Divine Revelation of Hell* (New Kensington, PA: Whitaker House, 1993).

Baxter, Mary K. *A Divine Revelation of the Spirit Realm* (New Kensington, PA: Whitaker House, 2000).

Baxter, Mary. "Stories of the SuperNatural," Interview. YouTube.com/watch?v=15Zvh7qCKJ0

Yeager, Michael. *Hell is For Real* (Michael Yeager).

Curtis "Earthquake" Kelley
"Boy Died of Drug Overdose and Went to Hell (Hell Testimony) Earthquake Kelley with Sid Roth," August 15, 2014, YouTube.

Mario Martinez
"Heaven vs. Hell: Mario Martinez sees hell, demons, angels and more, September 24, 2015, YouTube.

Ron Regan
"Atheist Died, Went to Hell, Came Back (Parts 1 and 2)," October 3, 2009, YouTube
"Hell Testimony, Ronald Reagan (Parts 1 and 2)", July 2, 2009, YouTube
"Near Death Experience, Man See Vision of Hell," Testimonial of Evangelist Ronald Reagan, December 8, 2008, YouTube

Choo Thomas
ChooThomas.org

Thomas, Choo. *Heaven is So Real!* (Lake Mary, FL: Charisma House, 2003).

Bernarda Fernandez
"Prepare for the Lord's Return," by Bernarda Fernandez, Audio, www.divinerevelations.info.
"5 Days in Heaven and Hell - Bernada Fernandez (sic)," January 11, 2014, YouTube.
Peralta, Mike. *Hell Testimonies* (Mike Peralta, 2012), Bernarda Fernandez.
Bernada Fernandez, Due Esperiencze vissute nell'al-dila con Gesu Cristo, [Two Experiences I Had with Jesus Christ in the hereafter], Parole de Vie, B.P. 3, 30920-Codognan (France), 1996, pages 10-16

DivineRevelations.info
Near-Death.com
GodEmbassy.com
www.worldometers.info/world-population
www.worldpopulationbalance.org
www.worldlifeexpectancy.com/live-world-death-to-tals
www.unicef.org/mdg/childmortality.html

Made in United States
Troutdale, OR
11/29/2023

15084042R00086